READING JESUS

Meeting the Word of God

VANCE L. TOIVONEN

The Bible is typically referred to as The Word of God. But before there even was something called The Bible there was The Word of God, a Living Word spoken through the Prophets and ultimately through Jesus of Nazareth, whose voice echoes down through the ages, through religions, through cultures and into the 21st century. So, the Bible may not be the Word of God after all.

iUniverse, Inc.
Bloomington

Reading Jesus
Meeting the Word of God

iUniverse books may be ordered through booksellers or by contacting:

iUniverse
1663 Liberty Drive
Bloomington, IN 47403
www.iuniverse.com
1-800-Authors (1-800-288-4677)

ISBN: 978-1-4759-0799-5 (sc)
ISBN: 978-1-4759-0801-5 (hc)
ISBN: 978-1-4759-0800-8 (ebk)

Printed in the United States of America

iUniverse rev. date: 04/09/2012

All biblical references are from Eugene H. Peterson, The Message: The Bible in Contemporary Language. Colorado Springs: NavPress, 2002 unless otherwise noted.

Contents

Preface

Why did I write this book when there are so many books about the Bible and Jesus? I wrote this book because I had to. It was in my gut longing to ooze out into the evolutionary ether of this world. I did not write this book for any kind of recognition; and certainly not with a goal of generating a revenue stream. My goal was to literally get The Word out.

I had a seminary professor who taught preaching. He told us that we would know the good news (the gospel) because when we experience it firsthand we will not be able to keep it to ourselves; we will not be able to hold it in. He said time and time again that it would "blow a hole in our throats." I felt that way about what I wrote here, no matter how well I wrote it, or how well received the book might be at the end of the day.

I have asked some close friends to read it, and they have given it their nod of approval, as well as provided me with apt editing suggestions. I will not name them all here, lest I leave one or two out; but I am grateful to you all (you know who you are). I would, however, like to give special thanks to Jim and Pat McGrane (Pat did the cover too) who encouraged and championed this book. If it were not for them I would not be writing these words, or any other words you will find herein.

The good news came for me when I realized that The Word of God was not a book, but a person. I noticed how all of the religious conflict around me seemed to be based upon how people use (and abuse) The Book (whether The Bible or The Koran). I felt there had to be a better way, a better foundation upon which to build my faith. Because I have grown up in the Christian religion, it seemed reasonable that Jesus of Nazareth would be a good choice. On my path I have studied other teachers (Buddha, Mohammed, Rumi, et al), but Jesus would give me more than enough to work on for the remainder of my earthly existence. So, Jesus it is. This book is about Jesus.

And speaking of books, I have chosen *The Message*, translation of The Bible by Eugene H. Peterson, as my preferred biblical text. You will also find Peterson reflected in this book in the form of quotes from his other writings. He has had a profound influence on me. I am thankful to Eugene H. Peterson for being a great pastor to this pastor. (By the way, Peterson's resent autobiography is titled *The Pastor: A Memoir*).

I prefer *The Message* because it speaks to me in the 21st century. If Jesus is to speak to us in the 21st century, then it helps if he speaks like a guy that actually lives in the 21st century (and I believe that he does). This is not easy work, taking a guy from the 1st century and transplanting him into the 21st century. Yet, that is what I need to do to help Jesus live in the context of my life; it is what I need to do in order to make him real to me, and not just a picture on the wall. I hope that through this process I can also help make him real to the people around me, the people I serve in my congregation, and the strangers that I meet. Eugene H. Peterson has helped me with this process; and not only me but millions of others who have discovered *The Message*, and his other writings.

I cannot find the actual reference in Martin Luther's writings, so I'm not really sure he ever said what I am about to say that he said. Many others have already done so (just Google it), but none that I have found have offered a reference. The quote attributed to Luther is, "The Bible is the cradle (or manger) wherein Christ is laid." For the person who claims to follow Jesus, as Christians by definition should, Jesus must be the centerpiece of the faith. The Bible is a tool, then, for focusing on that center—Jesus. This is why I wrote this book. I want to encourage people who already call themselves Christians to put Jesus first; and to perhaps invite others to take a second look at this guy from Nazareth too; this guy from 1ˢᵗ century Nazareth who now walks our streets and interacts with our 21ˢᵗ century world.

Introduction

On Sunday mornings I need to walk through several gathering places to get to my office to take off my robe and move into the next thing I need to do. I walk through the fellowship hall where people have gathered for coffee and conversation, then up the stairs and into a room that is filled with loud noises. It is the noise of young children singing; and on this particular morning not so much singing and yelling. They are singing a song but it sounds like they are at the local high school football game on a Friday night. The song they are yelling enthusiastically is:

The B-I-B-L-E. Yes, that's the book for me!
I stand alone on the Word of God, The B-I-B-L-E!

They love that song.

From a very young age we teach our children who grow up in Christian churches to associate the term *Word of God* with a book we call The Bible. As a pastor it is my job, I suppose, to make sure that they do this. After all, it is right there in my ordination vows.

> *The church in which you are to be ordained*
> *confesses that* **the Holy Scriptures are the word of God**
> *and are the norm of its faith and life.*
> *We accept, teach, and confess the Apostles', the Nicene, and the*
> *Athanasian Creeds.*
> *We also acknowledge the Lutheran Confessions*
> *as true witnesses and faithful expositions of the Holy Scriptures.*
> *Will you therefore preach and teach in accordance with the Holy*
> *Scriptures*
> *and these creeds and confessions?*
> *Each ordinand responds: I will, and I ask God to help me.*[1]

Those vows ask me to "preach and teach in accordance with the Holy Scriptures." But even the Holy Scriptures do not refer to the book we now call *The Bible* as the *Word of God*.

What the term "the Holy Scriptures" represents varies historically. In 2 Timothy we find the most direct reference to a written word of God in the New Testament.

> *But don't let it faze you. Stick with what you learned and believed,*
> *sure of the integrity of your teachers—why, you took in the sacred*
> *Scriptures with your mother's milk! There's nothing like the written*
> *Word of God for showing you the way to salvation through faith*
> *in Christ Jesus. Every part of Scripture is God-breathed and useful*
> *one way or another—showing us truth, exposing our rebellion,*
> *correcting our mistakes, training us to live God's way. Through the*

---

[1] Evangelical Lutheran Worship, Pew Edition copyright 2006, Augsburg Fortress, Publishers.

Word we are put together and shaped up for the tasks God has for
us. (2 Timothy 3:14-17)²

What were these scriptures for Timothy? Who wrote these words to Timothy? Well, the answer to those questions depends upon what tradition you find yourself in. If you are in a tradition that purports that The Bible as we know it today is the inerrant, infallible Word of God, then Paul wrote all of the epistles in the New Testament attributed to him. You would also claim undeniably that the first five books of The Bible were actually written by Moses.

However, if you are more inclined toward seeing The Bible as a book through which God can certainly speak, or if you are a so-called "liberal" scholar, then you are allowed to enter into educated dialogue with The Bible, question The Bible, conclude that Paul wrote some but not all of the epistles in the New Testament³, and claim with some certainty that Moses was not the prolific author that some allege him to have been. In short, you can wonder about The Bible's authority, which is exactly what James Barr does in his book *The Scope and Authority of the Bible.*

. . . the Bible has authority because its authority . . . is built into
the structure of the Christian faith and the Christian religion . . .
The Bible is more a battleground than a book of true facts . . .
In (Jesus') time there was already a scripture, and there was also
a religious tradition that sought to interpret that scripture. Jesus'

---

2   All biblical references are from Peterson, Eugene H. (2002). *The Message: The Bible in Contemporary Language.* Colorado Springs: NavPress unless otherwise noted.

3   Mack, Burton L. (1995). *Who Wrote the New Testament.* Harper, pp. 206-207.

> *dialogue with Jewish leaders probed into areas of problems that lay between the scripture and its alleged interpretation within the people of God; and, as the gospels depict it, it was this probing that led to the rejection of Jesus, his trial and crucifixion . . .[4]*

What people in various historical periods refer to as "scripture" varies historically, even as it varies today. A modern day Jew has a different "scripture" than an ancient Jew had. A Muslim has the Koran. A Hindu has the Bhagavad Gita. A Buddhist refers to the Tipitaka, or the Pali canon. What the author of Timothy referred to as "the written Word of God" had a certain canon of writing in mind, probably a blend of what we now call the Old Testament and some of the early versions of what came to be included in the New Testament writings we have today. In the next chapter I will look more closely at how what we call The Bible came to be just that.

However, this is not a book about The Bible. This is a book about the Word of God. I am far more interested in what that term means, or rather what I have come to discover that it means. It does not mean a book for me; at least not primarily or exclusively. Any authority attributed to The Bible does not reside in the book itself. The Bible is a pile of paper and ink and glue. I am writing this book because I think The Bible has value that far exceeds the printed page. I will contend that The Word of God is not a book at all. The Word of God has breath and life. The Word of God has flesh and blood. The Word of God is perhaps not just "a word" at all, if by word one means the collection of fonts I am using to communicate to you right now.

> *In talking about the essential implication of scripture in the process of salvation, in the life of the church, and in the faith of*

---

[4]   Barr, James (1980. The Scope and Authority of the Bible. Westminster, pp. 52-53

the Christian, we are not talking about 'accepting' the contents of the Bible or 'believing the Bible.' Christian faith is not faith in the Bible, not primarily; it is faith in Christ as the one through whom one comes to God, and faith that through the Bible we meet him, he communicates with us. The Bible is thus the instrument of faith and the expression of faith, rather than the object of faith.[5]

I have a beautiful guitar made from gorgeous Koa wood. When I picked it up from the music store the clerk who had received it in shipping and set it up for me said, "This is the most beautiful guitar we have ever had in the store." I do not play this guitar nearly enough (my son recently noticed dust on it and frowned at me for my neglect). To leave that beautiful guitar on its stand and to worship its beauty is to miss the point of having the guitar in the first place. But when I sing and play the guitar, when the guitar is used to communicate real meaning and offer reflective and meditative opportunities to the listeners, then the guitar lives; it has authority, if you will.

The same is true of any instrument. Anne Akiko Meyers, an acclaimed concert violinist, purchased a rare Stradivarius violin at auction for $3,600,000. The violin was originally in the collection of Napoleon Bonaparte. Around 500 Stradivarius violins still exist in the world. Now, one would think that the thing to do with such an instrument would be to put it in a museum with some very high tech security system. But Ms. Meyers plays her violin. I heard her play *Summertime* on a television news show. She played with passion, beauty and near perfection; her very being seeped through the bow and the strings of the violin. She communicated

---

[5]   Ibid, p. 55

life through that priceless instrument. It is the music that she made that offered life, not the instrument itself.

What I am inviting in this book is that we listen to the music that is being expressed in and through The Bible; and the primary music is for me, if you will, the One who sings the songs of hope and justice and light and peace—Jesus. But we will not hear this song if we become enamored with that pile of paper and ink and glue. We will not hear this song if we get sidetracked by legalistic arguments about what the Bible "says." The Bible doesn't "say" anything. The Bible cannot speak. It has no cardiovascular system; no heart, no lungs, no organs of any kind. The Bible has no ears, no eyes, no sense of taste or touch or smell. In order for the Bible to have any such animation it must be synthesized through flesh and blood; your flesh and mine; your blood and mine. We synthesize it any way we want. We can make the Bible part of our war chest, just as Bonaparte did with his Stradivarius collection; or we can make beautiful music with it. It is our choice, really. I will choose the latter.

Frederich Buechner has a lengthy section on the Bible in his theological ABC book, *Wishful Thinking*. Along the way he refers to Karl Barth's book *The Word of God and the Word of Men* paraphrasing that reading the Bible is like looking out through a window[6]

Buechner concludes the section,

> If you look at a window, you see fly-specks, dust, the crack where
> Junior's Frisbee hit it. If you look through a window, you see the
> world beyond. Something like this is the difference between those

---

[6]   Buechner, Frederich (1973). Wishful Thinking: A Theological ABC. Harper
       & Row, p. 9.

*who see the Bible as a Holy Bore and those who see it as the Word
of God which speaks out of the depths of an almost unimaginable
past into the depths of ourselves.*[7]

Reading the Bible will be a challenge, to be sure. But if all we do is look at it, or refer to it, like it was something in and of itself, we will ultimately miss the point of it altogether. It is my sincere hope that in writing this book I in no way discourage any of us from reading the Bible, but rather encourage us to read the Bible for what it is—an opportunity to encounter a Word of God that is living, breathing, and life-altering. I do not want anyone reading the Bible with the goal of changing other people, or altering the world around them. I want us to read the Bible with one primary goal in mind—to change ourselves; or rather, to let the One we meet through the Bible show us how to change.

*. . . to read the Scriptures adequately and accurately, it is necessary
at the same time to live them. Not to live them as a prerequisite to
reading them, and not . . . in consequence of reading them, but . . .
as we read them, the living and the reading reciprocal . . . It means
letting Another have a say in everything we are saying and doing.
It is as easy as that. And as hard.*[8]

For me the "Another" that Peterson refers to here is Jesus. With our broad interpretations of God we can fly all over the place. The term and the concept "God" is a huge, mysterious, gigantic notion. "God" is as vast a territory to explore as deep space itself. We live in the Milky Way; one solar system in one galaxy in a vast universe. Scientists are still trying to

---

[7]   Ibid, p. 12

[8]   Peterson, Eugene H. (2006). Eat This Book: A Conversation in the Art of Spiritual Reading. William B. Eerdmans, p. xii.

determine the number of galaxies that exist in the universe (something that we simply cannot currently conclude with absolute certainty). One NASA website estimates the number of galaxies at approximately 125 billion.[9] There are other estimates as great as 500 billion. Even if we take Hubble's evidence of 3,000 visible galaxies, each with perhaps 100 solar systems, there are at least 300,000 solar systems in the known universe; 300,000 groupings of planets orbiting a single star, like our Sun. That is enough, perhaps, for any of us to wrap our heads around before we start chattering away about "God." God is greater than the universe itself—greater than ll 3,000-500 billion possible galaxies. How do we begin to even fathom such a concept as God?

I do believe that God (or whatever anyone happens to call that possible intelligence behind the universe) speaks to us. God speaks through prophets and priests. God speaks through great expressions of wisdom like Ghandi, Martin Luther King Jr., and Mother Theresa. God speaks through poetry and music and art. For me, and for the two or so billion who claim Christianity as their religious preference, one of the primary conduits for God's "voice" is Jesus of Nazareth. I have heard John Dominic Crossan refer to Jesus as *God in sandals*. We can argue all day about what God is or is not. But Jesus, for one, brings God down to earth in a way that you and I can latch on to, leaving less room for speculation.

In the first chapter I will go over some of the history of how The Bible came to be The Word of God; as well as how the Bible came to be—period. Others have done this work. I am primarily borrowing from their work, stating historic fact, and wondering about what it means for those of us who read the book. The Bible is a book that has come to us only after

---

[9]   http://imagine.gsfc.nasa.gov/docs/ask_astro/answers/021127a.html

many centuries of negotiation and changes on the religious landscape of civilization. The Bible did not drop out of the sky, like that monolith at the beginning of *2001: A Space Odyssey*.[10] It is, like you and me, a conduit for God's voice in the world; a means through which God might, but does not always, speak.

In the second chapter my primary focus will be on the term "Word of God." What are its origins? How has it been variously used? Here I will flesh out the idea that the Word of God is better off not relegated to a book; that the Word of God is intended to be a living and breathing word. Here I will associate the Word of God with one particular expression of that word, while understanding and honoring the variety of ways in which that term is utilized. My goal is to suggest that reading The Bible as the Word of God without first listening to the living Word of God may result in—to say the least—trouble. That living Word of God is for me, Jesus.

The rest of the book will be dedicated to looking at a section of the fifth chapter of the gospel of Matthew where Jesus, the living Word of God, reinterprets scripture to the people of his time. I will then enter into some concluding commentary.

I hope you find this book helpful in your faith journey. It took me half a lifetime to get here. I guess I am a slow learner. I realize that the conclusions I draw here were acquired from a process, a long and sometimes perilous process. My apologies to anyone who was injured during this process, the many in communities I have served who sometimes looked at me and wondered what was up with that guy. I am no different than The

---

[10] 1968 film based on "The Sentinel" by Arthur C. Clarke (Written 1948, first published 1951 as "Sentinel of Eternity").

Bible itself. My life has pages and chapters that contain a wide variety of material. Again I turn to Buechner.

> *(The Bible) is a book about both the sublime and the unspeakable, it is a book also about life as it really is. It is a book about people who at one and the same time can be both believing and unbelieving, innocent and guilty, crusaders and crooks, full of hope and full of despair. In other words it is a book about us.*[11]

The same is true of you who so graciously hold this book in your hands. I pray with all my heart that this book will help you ultimately experience more of the sublime than the unspeakable. I hope that this book will encourage you to consider a deeper and more meaningful relationship with the Word of God—not the book, but the person—who is, for me, Jesus of Nazareth who lives in the words and memories of the people who have sought to follow him. I desire more than anything that this book will help other clergy and religious leaders to think twice before quoting scripture, and to let "Another" have a say, as Peterson put it so well. Mostly, that we never forget the real value of scripture, as the author of 2 Timothy put it, to "*show* us truth, *expose* our rebellion, *correct* our mistakes, and *train* us to live God's way."

---

[11]   Buechner, p. 9

Chapter One

THE BIBLE AND HOW WE GOT IT

(OR DIDN'T GET IT)

The Bible is the number one best-seller of all time. Walk into any bookstore and you will be confronted with a number of different translations, perhaps as many as two or three dozen. Globally the Bible is translated into hundreds of different languages. What a privilege it is to have so many choices. Prior to the sixteenth century people did not have such choices. The Reformation really began in earnest when Martin Luther defied Church authority by translating the Bible into German, the language of his people. Before that, the common people were dependent upon the interpretation of the priests and bishops who read the Bible only in Latin. But, did the translation of the Bible into common language make it any more widely read?

> *This German Bible (this is not praise for myself but the work praises itself) is so good and precious that it's better than all other versions, Greek and Latin, and one can find more in it than in all commentaries, for we are removing impediments and difficulties so that other people may read in it without hindrance. I'm only concerned that there won't be much reading in the Bible, for people are very tired of it and nobody clamors for it any more.*[12]

---

[12] Luther, M. (1999, c1967). Vol. 54: Luther's works, vol. 54 : Table Talk (J. J. Pelikan, H. C. Oswald & H. T. Lehmann, Ed.). Luther's Works (Vol. 54, Page 408). Philadelphia: Fortress Press.

The Bible is undoubtedly a bestseller because, like other books I have on my shelves, it is primarily a book we *intend* to read; or feel we *should* read. Before I take my last earthly breath I am certain that I will not have read every book that is currently cluttering up my home and office. Some I have read parts of, because sometimes parts are just as good as the whole thing. Some I think I *should* read, but probably never will. And some I have read and may read again.

A key thing about sacred scriptures is that at one time or another they existed in oral form. Stories like the two creation stories in Genesis were passed on to many generations before they were ever written down in some form or another. There are, then, a lot of changes that go into these stories and histories and poetries and letters before anyone ever gets to read them. It is not unlike the telephone game we play as children, whispering something into ear after ear until we finally hear the result on the other end of the line. Rarely do the two versions match.

A search on Amazon for history books about Abraham Lincoln resulted in 3,742 results. There must be some differences between these histories, otherwise there would be fewer to be sure. I am not a history buff, per se, but I would imagine that, if I were, I would read several of these histories and biographies of Lincoln and decide which one fits my particular slant on Lincoln. I would wish to make a case that Lincoln had something to say in the present, and therefore would lean toward the biography that best supported my bias.

Every author of written scripture ultimately used this same, very human method of decision-making. They wanted to make a point, to get their bias across to the reader. There are four gospels in the New Testament, each with their own agenda.[13] There are two creation stories in Genesis (Genesis 1:1-2:4 and Genesis 2:5-2:25), each with their own emphasis. The rest of the Bible is interpreted history, and artistic expression of the experiences of a people, experiences of a people with their God, or, to again use Crossan's reference, their experiences with "God in sandals."

So we tend to read the Bible in a way that supports our point of view. This is a perfectly natural tendency. In the Introduction to his very helpful book *How the Bible Became the Bible,* Donald L. O'Dell writes,

> *Most of us don't read the Bible. If we do, it's a verse here, three verses there. The Bible is not in a language we easily understand. It's dull and seems irrelevant. Besides, every time we've tried to read the Bible, we were confronted with all sorts of emotional baggage associated with Bible/church/religion that muddles the issue . . . So we don't read the Bible.*[14]

Perhaps you have felt this way. Perhaps this is the reason why you couldn't find a Bible in your house even if your life depended upon it. If you did find one, you might use it to stamp out a stove fire, or to squash a poisonous insect, or to knock out an intruder in your home. One of the things that might help in our approach to The Bible is to understand what it is; what it was meant to be in the first place. O'Dell continues.

> *I believe if we understand what the people of the Bible are trying to communicate, we can begin to see beyond their words, cultures,*

13 Shaia, Alexander J. (2010). The Hidden Power of the Gospels: Four Question, Four Paths, One Journey. Harper.
14 O'Dell, Donald L. (2006). How the Bible Became the Bible. Infinity Publishing, p. 7.

> *or history. When we've done that, we can see ourselves in them or, conversely, them in us. Then they become very real people and their experiences can relate to our experiences.*[15]

I had an experience with this right in the middle of a worship service. I had written my sermon on the gospel lesson from Luke chapter 6. I had given the first lesson a passing glance and the second lesson hardly a glance at all. But I totally ignored the Psalm, which we read responsively. It was Psalm 149, a coronation or kingly psalm, which began innocently enough.

> *Praise the LORD! Sing to the LORD a new song, his praise in the assembly of the faithful.*
> *Let Israel be glad in its Maker; let the children of Zion rejoice in their King.*
> *Let them praise his name with dancing, making melody to him with tambourine and lyre.*
> *For the LORD takes pleasure in his people; he adorns the humble with victory.*
> *Let the faithful exult in glory; let them sing for joy on their couches.*[16]

Those first five verses sounded like a party with music and dancing and perhaps a little wine and ale. Those first five verses sounded like something people could understand, like an evening at a wedding dance. The king is the centerpiece of this celebration, which we might need to translate into an inaugural ball in our American context. We get this. I was comfortable

---

[15] Ibid, p. 8.

[16] New Revised Standard Version Bible, copyright 1989, Division of Christian Education of the National Council of the Churches of Christ in the United States of America.

with those first five verses. I was all happiness and joy. But then, suddenly, there came the rest of the verses like a 20 mega-ton bomb.

> *Let the high praises of God be in their throats and two-edged swords in their hands,*
> *to execute vengeance on the nations and punishment on the peoples,*
> *to bind their kings with fetters and their nobles with chains of iron,*
> *to execute on them the judgment decreed. This is glory for all his faithful ones. Praise the LORD!*[17]

I sat there painfully aware that we were advocating for violence; that the "two-edged sword" was real; that the "punishment" and the "vengeance" were real; that the overthrow of other nations and their leaders was real. This was a celebration on the eve of going to war and executing judgment in the name of God. I was about to get up in the pulpit and preach about a Jesus who said "love your enemies" not "smote your enemies with a sword." There was no romanticizing of the text in that moment. The tension it created was real for me. How could I hold the Bible together without holding it in tension? How could I listen to the Bible without realizing that two very different agendas were being propagated this Sunday, and both of them in the Bible?

The Bible that we Christian folks hold in our hands has its genesis at the beginning of the first millennium B.C.E. The earliest author of the Old Testament is someone who has come to be referred to as "J" because this author referred to God as JHWH (also YHWH) which, when you add vowels, becomes Jawheh, or Yahweh.

---

[17] Ibid.

Next we have the author "E" who referred to God as Elohim, writing around the beginning of the second quarter of the first millennium. Then comes "D," the Deuternomist (around 625 B.C.E.), who primarily authored what we now call the book of Deuteronomy, where most of the laws and rules and regulations are; the legal code of the Old Testament. Finally there is "P," the Priestly author (around 400 B.C.E). The Priestly author has as a central focus the establishment of the Temple, and the cultic life of Israel.

Throw in the Prophets (Jeremiah, Isaiah, Amos, et al), the Wisdom literature (Psalms, Proverbs, Job, et al), and the Apocalyptic literature (Daniel) and you have the Old Testament written over the course of the first millennium B.C.E. That's a thousand years, or about fifteen or more lifetimes by the human standards of that time. We already have a mixed bag of literature here, and a variety of different authors and agendas. This is not a collection of literature intended to be monolithic. The Biblical literalist will insist this is just more evidence of the miraculous, that God could take such a diverse anthology and unify it in some way. Even the Jewish scholars and leaders could not ultimately do this. They decided to divide what we call the Old Testament into three different collections of literature—The Torah (first five books), the Prophets, and the Writings.[18]

The miracle, if there is one, is that we can somehow wade through this voluminous compilation and come to any kind of agreement about what in the world God seems to be doing, or wishes to do. The intentions of the authors may or may not jive with the objectives of the God of the Universe. Who can know such intentions with any certainty anyway? And

---

[18] O'Dell, p. 94.

yet somehow, sometimes we stumble upon a shred of light in the darkness. That is the Old Testament.

There are, by the way, inter-testamental books, sometimes called the Old Testament Apocrypha. Roman Catholics have some of these books in their canon. These too are divided up into different kinds of literature—historical books (1 Esdras, 2 Esdras (4 Ezra), Tobit, Judith, Judith Gets A Head of Holophernes, The Rest of Esther, 1 Maccabees), poetic books (The Wisdom of Solomon, Wisdom of Sirach, The Song Of The Three (Prayer of Azariah), Prayer of Manasseh), books of prophecy (Baruch, Daniel, Bell and the Dragon, Daniel and Susanna, Letter of Jeremiah), and other stuff (3 Maccabees, 4 Maccabees, Psalm 151, Testament of Job). All of these books were at some point canonized in the West, and all were composed in the later centuries of the first millennium, closer to the time Jesus walked the earth. There are many other books written during this period that were not chosen to be included in The Bible.

Canonization is the process whereby church leaders eventually determined that what you now hold in your hands and call *The Bible* is indeed *The Bible*. When it comes to the New Testament we have the same kind of sorting out to do. We have the four gospels, Acts, the Pauline letters (including the ones scholars do not agree on as having originated with Paul), the Pastoral epistles, the Catholic epistles, the Johannine letters, James and last but not least, Revelation. The earliest writers of the New Testament material were Paul, and an author referred to simply as 'Q;' but by far the very closest material to the actual, living, breathing Jesus of Nazareth was the material of the community that produced 'Q.'

Burton Mack has written an excellent book on the formation of the New Testament. If you read his book and O'Dell's book you will have some pretty helpful information about the creation of the Bible. I am particularly interested in Mack's overview of the early Jesus movements. Before there was anything called Christianity there were Jesus movements. Mack tells us one of those Jesus movements was the Community of Q. Of this community he writes,

> *Q will put us in touch with the earliest followers of Jesus. It is the earliest written record we have from the Jesus movement, and it is a precious text indeed . . . Q puts us as close to the historical Jesus as we will ever be.*[19]

Matthew and Luke used the earliest gospel (Mark) as their source, but also drew from Q (Q comes from the German Quella, meaning *source*). Mark was written around 80 C.E., Matthew around 90 C.E., and Luke and John's gospels at the turn of the century or later. Scholars vary in their dating of the gospels, but by any stretch these books were written after many decades of distance from the actual presence of Jesus on the planet. And remember, Paul's original letters predate the writing of the gospels.

What I am trying to do is provide you with a cursory overview of this material. The New Testament is pieced together from fragments, portions culled from over a century of writing. There are literal fragments, too; manuscripts that vary in their content, even down to specific passages that vary from one manuscript to another. Translating this material is like trying to put together a jigsaw puzzle with more pieces than will actually fit in the puzzle; the translator has to choose one piece over another.

---

[19]   Mack, p. 47.

Canonization does not occur until much later, after Christianity is firmly institutionalized and the Church has become a socio-political organization. The canonization of the Bible occurs in this crucible of religion and politics, finally giving birth to what we now call *The Bible* in the very late fourth century. Four centuries of negotiation, of "should we put this in or should we leave this out" lapsed before the Bible became one singular book—fourteen hundred years in the making. The Bible you hold in your hands is a collection that, for various reasons, people who called themselves Christian in the Fourth century thought we needed to have in our dossier.

There are other books too, the New Testament Apocrypha written concurrent with the material we find in the canonical New Testament, a complete list of which may be found here.[20] This is all material about Jesus, and all stuff that sounds biblical. One of my favorites is the Infancy Gospel of Thomas. Once Jesus developed into a God-man in the later gospels, it is only natural to wonder what he might have been like as a kid. Here is the third story from the second Greek version of this infancy narrative.

> *And Jesus made of that clay twelve sparrows, and it was the Sabbath. And a child ran and told Joseph, saying: Behold, thy child is playing about the stream, and of the clay he has made sparrows, which is not lawful. And when he heard this, he went, and said to the child: Why dost thou do this, profaning the Sabbath? But Jesus gave him no answer, but looked upon the sparrows, and said: Go away, fly, and live, and remember me. And at this word they flew, and went up into the air. And when Joseph saw it, he wondered.[21]*

---

[20] http://www.interfaith.org/christianity/apocrypha/new-testament-apocrypha/
[21] Infancy Gospel of Thomas, passage 3.

I also need to include the Gospel of Thomas, here (not to be confused with the Infancy Gospel of Thomas). The Gospel of Thomas comes from one of those earliest of Jesus movements, called the True Disciples. The Gospel of Thomas, like Q, is a series of Jesus sayings, with no narrative to speak of. The Gospel of Thomas was discovered among the Nag Hammadi library buried in a sealed jar and found by a peasant named Muhammad Ali Samman near the town of Nag Hammadi in Egypt in 1945. In his introduction to Stevan Davies' translation of the Gospel of Thomas, Andrew Harvey writes, "The Gospel of Thomas is, I believe, the clearest guide we have to the vision of the world's supreme mystical revolutionary, the teacher known as Jesus."[22]

The Gospel of Thomas (along with Q), writes Robert W. Funk, "permit us to reconstruct, to a limited extent, what the religion *of* Jesus must have been—as distinguished from the religion *about* Jesus, conceived by his first followers and amplified by Paul."[23] All of this is to say that whether we are reading within the canon (The Bible) or outside the canon (extra-biblical literature) we must make choices about what to pay attention to and how to interpret everything else. Canon or no canon we have a whole lot of material to wade through. How do we read that material? How do we even begin to figure out how the texts we consume interact with our everyday lives? With our culture? With our world? With our politics? With ourselves?

We can go to church and listen to preacher after preacher, but they are only processing the texts from their points of view. What about your

---

[22] Davies, Stevan (2002). The Gospel of Thomas Annotated & Explained, Translated and annotated by Stevan Davies; Forward by Andrew Harvey. Skylight Paths Publishing, p. x.

[23] Funk, Robert W. (1996). Honest to Jesus. Harper, p. 41.

point of view? The only reason, it seems, to tackle this material at all is to make adjustments to our points of view. It is certainly not just to find supporting material for our existing points of view. That is material that is culturally available for us 24/7 on cable news, talk radio, or your favorite religious programming. No, as the author of 2 Timothy set out, this material, whatever we happen to call our scriptures, or holy books, is intended for the purpose of *showing us truth, exposing our rebellion, correcting our mistakes, and training us to live God's way.*

> *We open this book and find that page after page it takes us off guard, surprises us, and draws us into its reality . . . receiving the words in such a way that they become interior to our lives, the rhythms and images becoming practices of prayer, acts of obedience, ways of love.*[24]

No matter how these writings, canon or no canon, came to be available to us, I am discovering that the real value of these writings is not in the pursuit of theological proofs, but in the process of intrapersonal reformation. Here I find out how far I live from the kingdom of God Jesus kept inviting people to enter into. Here I discover that it is not nuclear weaponry or military might that energizes the world, but rather divine and uncompromising love. Here I learn that what I see when I turn on the TV news is not reality from God's point of view, but some sort of weird alternate reality that God is longing to break through and have a voice in.

One summer day at a local ballgame I was talking with one of my parishioners only to discover that she was a fan of Glenn Beck. I am, admittedly, not a fan of the man so we entered into a back and forth

---

[24]   Eugene H. Peterson, Eat This Book: A Conversation in the Art of Spiritual Reading (William B. Eerdmans, 2006) pp. 6-11.

conversation. Realizing after a few minutes of friendly banter that neither of us was going to succeed at convincing the other of their point of view I ended the conversation by suggesting that for every hour that she spends listening to Glenn Beck, she spend a comparable hour listening to Jesus, reading his words and stories. How many of us give equal time to the living Word of God; that is to say, to Jesus, in this way?

There are myriad voices that pour into my consciousness and yours every day through television, radio, the Internet, magazines and newspapers. The Bible is a collection of voices also longing to grab our attention just long enough to recommend their points of view. I say "points of view" because the Bible does not speak with a singular point of view. Rather, the Bible somehow congeals its diversity of voices into a marvelous stew that says at the end of the day that God has the best interest of the whole creation in mind (not just human beings, by the way).

In the chapters ahead I will suggest that One voice in particular is the voice I choose to pay the most attention to; the voice whose point of view matters most in all of scripture to me; the voice that guides and directs my life when I am at my best, and the voice we need so desperately to find time for in our busy and over-saturated lives. This voice is the primary processing tool for making sense of scripture for me, for picking through the stew and discerning its ingredients, and for discovering God's voice somehow in the midst of all of the other voices that jockey for our attention, even in the Bible. Burton Mack shares his vision.

My own fantasy is to enter a hall and find high ceilings, lovely chandeliers, walls lined with bookshelves, wines in the alcove, hors d'oeuvres by the windows, and a wide table down the middle of the room with the Bible sitting on it. And there we are, all of us,

*walking around, sitting at the table, and talking about what we
should do with that book . . . Everyone has been invited . . . There
are historians of religion, cultural anthropologists, and political
scientists, but also politicians, CEOs, and those who work in foreign
affairs. The ethnic communities of Los Angeles County are all well
represented, as are women, the disenfranchised, the disabled, and
all the voiceless . . . Merchants are there, and workers, and airline
pilots . . . everyone gets to talk and ask questions. No one has a
corner on what the Bible says. We blow whistles if anyone starts
to pout or preach. What we are trying to figure out is why we
thought the Bible so important, whether it is so important, how
it has influenced our culture, what we think of the story . . . how
it fits or does not fit our current situation, and whether the story
should be revised in keeping with our vision of a just, sustainable,
festive, and multicultural world. Wouldn't that be something?*[25]

What a wonderful reminder that the Book is not just for our personal
use. The Bible, if it has any value at all, is a book that speaks to real life
not only where you and I live it, but where the billions on this planet also
live their lives; some of them barely living at all. In other words, the Bible
is not just a personal self-help book. It is not about me and God and no
one else. It is about God and us, all of us, every living thing on the planet.
The Bible is about creation itself. And all of that creation is represented
somehow, some way, in the great diversity of voices telling their stories of
life with the God expressed in the Bible.

When I come to Burton Mack's "wide table" I will bring with me the
bias I will be expressing in the pages of this book. I will bring my Jesus

---

[25]   Mack, p. 310.

bias, just as the Buddhist will bring her Buddha bias and the Muslim her Muhammad bias. There will be the Hindu with his many gods, and the Jew with her devotion to one God. There we will stand together with respect for one another and listen to one another as we seek common footing for walking together in this world. Without this kind of respect we will never capture the bold vision of the Bible, or any of our various Holy Scriptures. I hope to show that Jesus sought to engender this kind of respect, and to lead us toward a more peaceful existence, even with our so-called enemies.

The Word of God is the Word of God only when it speaks; only when it has voice. Can it be the Word of God if no one hears it? If a Bible falls out of a tree in the forest, does anyone hear it? The book cannot speak. Only the voices in the book can speak; and that one most essential voice—Jesus' voice can certainly speak. This is the voice I will encourage us to listen to in this book.

Chapter Two

THE WORD IS THE WORD

It never really made any sense to me. I don't think it was intended to. After all, it was written and performed in the early 1960s by a group called The Trashmen. The song "Surfin' Bird" declares that "The bird is the word" and that "Everybody's heard about the bird." Oh, and let's not forget the most important lyric, "Papa oom mow mow, papa oom mow mow."[26] As one surfs the internet today (a kind of surfing The Trashmen never could have imagined when they wrote the song), one finds that the interpretation of this 1963 lyric has grown to be quite obscene. We live in a culture where the use of the term "the bird" has taken on a totally different connotation. But a little historical research enlightened me to the fact that The Trashmen were merely referring to a dance that was popular at the time, a dance called "the bird."

The term "Word of God" has also gone through various historical meanderings and cultural reinterpretations. Today it is widely used to refer to a book called The Bible, as that children's song and the ordination vows pointed out in the introduction to this book. In other words, "The Word of God" has not always been a term used to reference the Bible we are now familiar with. In fact, it has not always been used to refer to a book at all.

---

[26]   Surfin' Bird © Beechwood Music Corporation

In this chapter I will cover variations in the usage of the term, and suggest that I have a definite bias as to how I prefer to use the term.

Let's begin in the beginning with the first creation story in Genesis.

First this: God created the Heavens and Earth—all you see, all you don't see. Earth was a soup of nothingness, a bottomless emptiness, an inky blackness. God's Spirit brooded like a bird above the watery abyss.

> *God spoke: "Light!"*
> *And light appeared . . .*

> *God spoke: "Sky! In the middle of the waters;*
> *separate water from water!"*
> *God made sky . . .*

> *God spoke: "Separate!*
> *Water-beneath-Heaven, gather into one place;*
> *Land, appear!"*
> *And there it was . . .*

> *God spoke: "Lights! Come out!*
> *Shine in Heaven's sky!*
> *Separate Day from Night.*
> *Mark seasons and days and years,*
> *Lights in Heaven's sky to give light to Earth."*
> *And there it was . . .*

> *God spoke: "Swarm, Ocean, with fish and all sea life!*
> *Birds, fly through the sky over Earth!"*

God created the huge whales,
    all the swarm of life in the waters,
And every kind and species of flying birds . . .

God spoke: "Earth, generate life! Every sort and kind:
    cattle and reptiles and wild animals—all kinds."
And there it was . . .

God spoke: "Let us make human beings in our image, make them
    reflecting our nature
So they can be responsible for the fish in the sea,
    the birds in the air, the cattle,
And, yes, Earth itself,
    and every animal that moves on the face of Earth."
God created human beings. (Genesis 1:27).

The ancients who used this story to explain the origins of the world had a particular bias not only *that* God created the world, but also *how* God created the world. God spoke the world into existence. The Word of God, meted out here in simple commands; *"Light!" "Sky!" "Separate!" "Come out!" "Swarm!" "Generate!"* is what brings into reality that which was *"a soup of nothingness, a bottomless emptiness, an inky blackness."* The Word of God is set out at the beginning of the Bible to be a tool that is used to create, to bring into existence that which does not previously exist.

The next time we encounter the phrase Word of God is in the 15th chapter of Genesis. Abram (He had not yet become Abraham), had just returned from great success in battle. The king wanted to reward him, but Abram refused because he did not want the king to "own" him, he did not want to be indebted to the king. His allegiance was to God and God alone. It

17

is at this point that God speaks to Abram. God has been speaking quite frequently to all of the characters in Genesis up to this point; to Adam and Eve, to Cain, to Noah (I can't help but be reminded of Bill Cosby's wonderful comedy routine on Noah), and now to Abram. But this is the first time the text uses the term "word of God."

> *After all these things, this **word of God** came to Abram in a vision: "Don't be afraid, Abram. I'm your shield. Your reward will be grand!" Abram said, "God, Master, what use are your gifts as long as I'm childless and Eliezer of Damascus is going to inherit everything?" Abram continued, "See, you've given me no children, and now a mere house servant is going to get it all."*

> *Then God's Message came: "Don't worry, he won't be your heir; a son from your body will be your heir." Then he took him outside and said, "Look at the sky. Count the stars. Can you do it? Count your descendants! You're going to have a big family, Abram!" And he believed! Believed God! God declared him "Set-Right-with-God. (Genesis 15:1-6).*

There is a verse tossed into Genesis chapter 4, the very last verse to be exact, that reads, *"That's when men and women began praying and worshiping in the name of God."* This would suggest to me that the author was explaining the beginnings of a practice that was already in place, the practice of some sort of cultic Yahweh worship. Within the context of that worship it is likely that stories were told, that "scripture" was used. It is quite probable that people heard such words as words from God, as the Word of God. So there we have it, the early origins of re-iterating God's word and calling it the Word of God.

Moses is the first real God translator, I suppose. He would go up to the mountain, encounter and speak with God, then return to the people to deliver the message. One such message is recorded in the first chapter of Deuteronomy, one of a series of sermons Moses delivered to Israel. The message sounds much like the prophets yet to come in Israel's history.

> *Because of you God's anger spilled over onto me. He said, "You aren't getting in either. Your assistant, Joshua son of Nun, will go in. Build up his courage. He's the one who will claim the inheritance for Israel. And your babies of whom you said, 'They'll be grabbed for plunder,' and all these little kids who right now don't even know right from wrong—they'll get in. I'll give it to them. Yes, they'll be the new owners. But not you. Turn around and head back into the wilderness following the route to the Red Sea. (Deuteronomy 1:37-40).*

Then Moses says, "*I told you but you wouldn't listen. You rebelled at the plain word of God.*" There's that pesky word "listen." The term "word of God" is reference here to a living word, spoken through a human medium. It is a word that has flesh and bones on it. The word of God throughout the remainder of the Old Testament is always a word that comes to someone and through someone. Somehow the word of God comes—through a dream (2 Samuel 7:4), or directly, although I haven't a clue how these people heard the voice of God. Nevertheless, it is not something written in a book, but translated in real time through real people. For those who spoke God's words, the prophets and others, this was no different than you or I telling someone else what we heard a friend or a neighbor say, what we heard on the newscast last night, or what we heard an actor say during the viewing of a film or a TV show. We speak other people's words all of the time. These just happen to be God's words.

Now we get back to the telephone game. Our re-telling of other people's words inevitably involves some sort of 'spin' on our parts. We cannot help but influence the words of others, simply by the very fact that it is no longer the other who is speaking. The words sound different through us. Even the best actors color the words of the characters they're playing, because no matter how good they are or how hard they try, it is now a word being spoken through them. We compliment actors by telling them that we forgot it was them and believed it to be the actual character we were watching. Sir Ben Kingsley becomes Gandhi for us. Morgan Freeman becomes Nelson Mandela for us. But if we get out news footage of the same speeches and compare them side by side, there is likely to be a slight difference in time, an almost imperceptible set of variants that distinguish the performer from the real thing.

So it is with God's word. Throughout history people have claimed to speak God's word. But that word is ultimately colored by the character of the speaker. It is unavoidable. Still, somehow, God speaks. This is the miracle, the wonder. Through very human and broken people God continues to create through words, just as God spoke and created in the beginning when stars exploded and nebulae erupted into the wonder that is the universe. What we have in the Bible is people's words about The Word. To translate and speak (or re-speak) these words we must, to use Walter Brueggemann's term, *re-text* the texts.[27] We must let the Word encounter us in the present in the same way that the Word encountered those who heard it in the past. We must take their context for hearing it and juxtapose it with our context so that the Word can be spoken and create a new reality in our midst, a God-reality in our current situation.

---

[27] Brueggemann, Walter (2010). The Word That Redescribes the World. Fortress, pp.36ff.

This perspective requires that we submit our modernist rationalistic assumptions to the text and, even when the text sounds in violence and all of its unbearable harshness or other objectionable cadences, still to assume that engagement with this text is a primal engagement out of which comes missional energy, imagination, and identity. To be sure, such engagement with the text does not consist in blind acceptance of the text . . . such engagement makes possible a new field of courage and freedom.[28]

It is that lack of blind acceptance of the text that leads me to the Word of God, to the One that I consider to be, for me, the primary *re-texting* tool. We turn now to the New Testament, and a passage that echoes the first chapter of Genesis.

> *The Word was first,*
>> *the Word present to God,*
>> *God present to the Word.*
>
> *The Word was God,*
>> *in readiness for God from day one.*
>
> *Everything was created through him;*
>> *nothing—not one thing!—*
>> *came into being without him.*
>
> *What came into existence was Life,*
>> *and the Life was Light to live by.*

---

[28] Ibid, p. 37

> *The Life-Light blazed out of the darkness;*
>> *the darkness couldn't put it out . . .*

> *The Word became flesh and blood,*
>> *and moved into the neighborhood.*

> *We saw the glory with our own eyes,*
>> *the one-of-a-kind glory,*
>> *like Father, like Son,*

> *Generous inside and out,*
>> *true from start to finish. (John 1:1-5, 14)*

The Word of God is in John's gospel not a book at all. The Word of God is Jesus in John's gospel. For the Gnostic community that produced John's gospel Jesus was the embodiment of God's Word, the one who spoke most clearly God's intention. Jesus was at creation, and according to John's gospel participated in creation in the beginning. By the time John's gospel is written Jesus has become synonymous with God. When Jesus speaks, God speaks. When Jesus heals, God heals. This was not true of earlier Jesus communities who saw Jesus as very human. What we have in the other canonized gospels is a kind of God-man, a blend of the two traditions. I do not find it particularly comforting that Jesus becomes synonymous with God, but it happened and has become part of our Christian tradition. What Jesus is, for me, is the way I come to access God, to capture a glimpse of God. Jesus is how I get a clue regarding something about which I would otherwise be considerably clueless.

> *Jesus is for Christians the decisive revelation of God . . . Jesus reveals,*
> *discloses what can be seen of God in a human life and what a life*

filled with God looks like . . . For Christians, the decisive revelation
of God is a person. As son of God, he reveals God; as the Word become
flesh, he embodies what can be seen of God in a human life.[29]

Jesus then becomes the way to access and interpret all of the material that involves God, all of the words that are spoken about God, from ancient times to the present. Jesus becomes for the Christian a sort of filter through which all of the God-talk in religion and culture is synthesized. Without Jesus we will find it difficult to have any real focus, just as the Buddhist would find it difficult to focus without the teachings of the Buddha or an examination of his life. We all need some place where the buck stops, so to speak. For me, that place is Jesus.

If the Word of God is Jesus, what do we do with the Bible? What is the Bible if it is not the Word of God? And if the Bible is not the Word of God, what shall I do with my ordination vows?

Of course, Christians also speak of the Bible as the revelation of
God, indeed as the "Word of God." Yet orthodox Christian theology
from ancient times has affirmed that the decisive revelation of God
is Jesus. The Bible is "the Word" become words, God's revelation in
human words; Jesus is "the Word" become flesh, God's revelation in
a human life. Thus Jesus is more decisive than the Bible.[30]

Borg goes on to clarify that Jesus does not embody all of God. As I said earlier, if God is somehow greater than the universe which could have over 500 billion galaxies in it, any human being, even Jesus, can only capture

---

[29]   Borg, Marcus J.(2006). Jesus: Uncovering the Life, Teachings, and Relevance of a Religious Revolutionary. Harper, p. 6

[30]   Ibid, pp. 6-7

a glimpse of God's immensity. Still, Jesus does this as well as anyone else I know (or am still getting to know). Remember, the term "Word of God" is a living word that needs to be heard.

> *The use of the phrase the Word of God as a description of the Bible did not come into play until after the Protestant Reformation (in the 1500s). Neither Martin Luther nor John Calvin, the two pillars of Protestant theology, referred to scripture as the Word of God. That phrase was reserved only as a description of Jesus. When viewed within the time frame of the last 2,000 years, the phenomenon of referring to the Bible as the Word of God occurred rather recently.[31]*

I think we need to start moving away from thinking of the Bible as a monolithic Word of God. We need to stop giving every word in the Bible "authority" as if the words themselves were God. The way to move away from this penchant for Bibliolatry is to center ourselves in the One who can give us perspective on the book. That one, for Christians anyway, is Jesus.

My life has gone through several re-incarnations. I was raised in the Missouri Synod Lutheran Church, confirmed in the Wisconsin Synod Lutheran Church, and ordained into the American Lutheran Church by a Missouri Synod pastor in a Missouri Synod church. I was quite involved in the Charismatic movement, the Neo-Pentecostalism that captured many disenchanted mainline folks in the 1970s. This was during my high school and college years. In college I sang on gospel outreach teams, and even travelled to the Samoan Islands in that endeavor. Somewhere along the way I acquired a blue pin with white letters on it that declared, "Jesus

---

[31] O'Dell, p. 236

is My Lord." At the time I considered it a badge of honor, and wore it with pride. I'm not sure Jesus actually was my Lord at the time, but I at least thought that he was.

I entered seminary somewhat disillusioned, burned out from all of the hyper-religious activity of my earlier years. The "Jesus is My Lord" pin was relegated to a box, and remained in storage for at least thirty years. It wasn't until my journey to the far edges of the Christian faith, and a real loss of that faith, that I came in contact with that pin once again. I was teaching a class called 'Saving Jesus'[32] at a time when Jesus had become a dirty word for me. Jesus had been abused and co-opted by people to the religious right who were not really acting so much like Jesus; people like Rev. Fred Phelps who spewed hatred and vitriol upon people who are gay and lesbian and the variety of other ways nature expresses diversity. I became familiar with him when I acted in the play *The Laramie Project* about a young man who was literally left to die on a fence post in the dead of winter because he was "different." This is not a Jesus I was able to resonate with, much less have him be some sort of leader in my life.

The process of teaching that class, and opening my life to the "real" Jesus who lived and died on this planet, renewed my faith and brought me to Jesus as my center; to Jesus as my bottom line. I dug out that pin and placed it on my office desk because, perhaps for the first time in my life, I was actually willing to begin letting Jesus be the lord of my life. I found myself tugging at my Lutheran roots a bit, roots that shied away from so-called "decision" theology. I began to realize that following Jesus *is* a conscious decision. This following has little or nothing to do, in my mind, with what happens to me when I die, but rather what happens with me

---

[32] www.livingthequestions.com

while I am living in the here and now. The Word of God has something to say about that; much to say about that, and it was time for me to start listening to that Word; to my Lord Jesus.

> *I think it is important to look deeply into every act and every teaching of Jesus during his lifetime, and to use this as a model for our own practice. Jesus lived exactly as He taught, so studying the life of Jesus is crucial to understanding His teaching. For me, the life of Jesus is His most basic teaching, more important than even faith in the resurrection or faith in eternity.*[33]

It is one thing to *believe in* Jesus; it is quite another thing to *follow* Jesus; the latter is far more difficult and not particularly conducive to filling church pews. Orthodox Christian faith has put more emphasis on the believing part than on the following part; because, I think, it is frankly more marketable; at least this has been my experience growing up in Lutheranism and being theologically educated in a Lutheran seminary. The gospel of Matthew closes with what has been call The Great Commission.

> *Jesus, undeterred, went right ahead and gave his charge: "God authorized and commanded me to commission you: Go out and train everyone you meet, far and near, in this way of life, marking them by baptism in the threefold name: Father, Son, and Holy Spirit. Then instruct them in the practice of all I have commanded you. I'll be with you as you do this, day after day after day, right up to the end of the age." (Matthew 28:18-20).*

Thich Nhat (1995). Living Buddha, Living Christ. Riverhead Books,

In most mainline Christian churches we baptize first and train later. This is not the practice encouraged by Jesus here, and it was not the practice of the earliest Jesus followers. But whether we decide to follow Jesus before or after baptism is not the issue here. The issue is, when are we going to decide, to consciously choose to follow Jesus and to practice all he has commanded us? As a Jesus follower, who happens to be a leader in the church, a pastor, how can I lead the people if they do not all choose to follow Jesus. Truth be told, I think the vast majority of us, including yours truly, want to follow Jesus but simply find it difficult to do so. We are torn apart by so many different loyalties, and divided by the factionalism that is so prevalent in our society, in our politics, and in our religious institutions. Some watch FOX and some watch MSNBC. Barak Obama's Red State and Blue State speech that I found so inspirational in 2004 has gotten lost in the political wrangling of our time. Do you remember it?

> *Now even as we speak, there are those who are preparing to divide us, the spin masters, the negative ad peddlers who embrace the politics of anything goes.*

> *Well, I say to them tonight, there is not a liberal America and a conservative America—there is the United States of America. There is not a Black America and a White America and Latino America and Asian America—there's the United States of America.*

> *The pundits, the pundits like to slice-and-dice our country into Red States and Blue States; Red States for Republicans, Blue States for Democrats. But I've got news for them, too:*

> *We worship an awesome God in the Blue States, and we don't like federal agents poking around in our libraries in the Red States.*

> *We coach Little League in the Blue States and yes, we've got some gay friends in the Red States.*

> *There are patriots who opposed the war in Iraq and there are patriots who supported the war in Iraq.*[34]

We have chosen the politics, and the religion, of divisiveness. In the ELCA, the denomination in which I serve, over 400 congregations have voted to leave the ELCA since the decision was made in the summer of 2009 to allow openly gay and lesbian pastors to serve in the ELCA.[35] Jesus, as far as I know, has nothing, absolutely nothing, to say about this issue; and yet, all of these congregations have chosen to risk the value of a united community for the sake of a divisive socio-political issue. These congregations have divided themselves up into Red People and Blue People instead of focusing on being Jesus' people, Jesus followers. Some have used the Bible and quoted it, bypassing Jesus' teaching for obscure referencing and legalistic rants. I am saddened that people who are members of my religious community have made such choices, and I wonder who has more to do with this trend. Is it the media that blasts away at these issues? What would be different if we listened to Jesus first and Rush Limbaugh, Glenn Beck, or even Rachel Maddow, second?

I suppose it is my weariness of such pretentiousness that leads me to write down my thoughts in book form and to point us toward a better way to process our diversity. The Word is still the Word, no matter what diversions may distract us. The Bible is still just a book, no matter how

---

[34] Excerpted from Barack Obama's speech at the 2004 Democratic National Convention.
[35] http://209.157.64.200/focus/f-religion/2549744/posts, religion post by David Barnhart, July 7, 2010.

many times we may quote from it to support our own biases, fears, and agendas. The words in the Bible only live when they live in and through us. They were never intended to be objective. They were intended to be words we embody, words that live in and through us.

My task is to bring into awareness and focus . . . that this Scripture text . . . pulls us into revelation and welcomes us as participants in it . . . Christians don't simply learn or study or use Scripture; we assimilate it, take it into our lives in such a way that it gets metabolized into acts of love.[36]

You may be able to accomplish the remarkable task of tackling the entire Bible without a guide. I need Jesus for this. I need Jesus to be my commentator, my critic, my analyst, my guru, my director, my life-coach, and the primary interpretive tool with which I come to the task of reading the Bible. Without his guidance I will find myself lost in a sea of material so deep I might very well drown in it. I would say the same thing if I were a Buddhist. I would not read anything, including the Bible, without the guidance of the Buddha. One Muslim can read the Qur'an and find justification for flying planes into towers, killing over 3,000 people; while another Muslim will listen to the voice of Muhammad as a guide for interpreting the material in the book and know the path to peace is not a violent path.

[Allah] has revealed to me that you should adopt humility so that no one oppresses another. (Riyadh-us-Salaheen, Hadith 1589).

Anyone who believes in God and the Last Day should not harm his neighbor. Anyone who believes in God and the Last Day should

---

[36] Peterson, Eugene H. (2006). Eat This Book: A Conversation in the Art of Spiritual Reading. William B. Eerdmans, p. 18

entertain his guest generously. And anyone who believes in God and the Last Day should say what is good or keep quiet. (Sahih Al-Bukhari, Volume 8, Book 73, Number 47).

Even as the fingers of the two hands are equal, so are human beings equal to one another. No one has any right, nor any preference to claim over another. You are brothers. (Final Sermon of Muhammad).

By quoting the Bible and the Qur'an without the guidance of their earthly leaders, Jesus and Muhammad, both religions have strayed from their true calling, to bring peace and justice to the world through non-violent means. Gandhi took the best of these teachers and stood up to the British Empire without striking one blow. This is the kind of guidance that Jesus can provide, if we will avail ourselves of that guidance. If not, then we will choose our path, and likely find justification somewhere in the Bible for that path, so broad is the content of the book. But with Jesus there is simply not as much elbow room to entertain our own egos. This book is about listening to a living Word that challenges us to confront our own egos and agendas where they keep us from letting the Word of God dwell in us, and in our lives. That Word of God is the One I am recommending that we invite as *The* Word of God for us—Jesus.

There are hymns in our worship book in the ELCA that refer to the Bible as the Word of God; but I came across the following hymn and have been using it in worship quite often ever since. The hymn is titled *Word of God, Come Down to Earth*. The lyric suggests nothing of a book. I will close this chapter with the lyric to this hymn.

Word of God, come down to earth, living rain from heav'n descending; touch our hearts and bring to birth faith and hope and love unending.

Word almighty, we revere you; Word made flesh, we long to hear you. Word eternal, throned on high, Word that brought to life creation, Word that came from heav'n to die, crucified for our salvation, saving Word, the world restoring, speak to us, your love outpouring. Word that speaks God's tender love, one with God beyond all telling, Word that sends us from above God the Spirit, with us dwelling, Word of truth, to all truth lead us; Word of life, with one bread feed us.[37]

---

[37] Text: James Quinn, SJ born 1919.

Chapter Three

A Good Jewish Boy from Nazareth

I now live in a small town in Iowa; a town with a population under 1,000. We are Protestants and Catholics. I don't think there are any other religions represented here. I have yet to meet a Jewish person in town, for instance. I love almost everything about living in a small, rural community; not least of all the strong sense of community. I love the warmth and feeling of "we're all in this together." But there is one thing that one relinquishes when living in a small, rural Midwestern town: the diversity of the city. Some people prefer to be away from the diversity, but I miss it.

I barely tolerate the commentary about people who are "other." I will confront outright slander and racial bigotry if I hear it, (and I do hear it). Mostly I just want to remind people as often as possible that Jesus was Jewish. In fact, most of the people who first followed Jesus were Jewish.

Jesus' earliest followers—Peter, and Mary Magdelene, James and John, Joanna and Matthew—were, like Jesus himself, Jews. This designation signals not only their identification with the people of Israel but also their participation in a common set of practices and beliefs . . . But when the man for whom they had given up their livelihoods, their homes, their families—the man they believed to be God's anointed one, the Messiah—was nailed to the cross, their personal loyalty, social vision, and theological convictions were tested; with the proclamation of his resurrection, those loyalties, visions, and convictions were transformed.[38]

Whatever happened to Jesus post-resurrection, whatever he "becomes," the Jesus who walked the earth was Jewish, as were the people who followed him. This is an undeniable fact. Growing up in the Midwestern United States in the late 20th century as I did, and having no contact with the Jewish community, I am ill-equipped to understand this man who grew up in Nazareth in the early first century. Furthermore, I am unfamiliar with the Galilean culture Jesus was nurtured in as a young boy. So I have at least two strikes against me before I ever attempt to read about what Jesus said, what he taught, and how he responded to the people around him in real time. It is all so—well—foreign.

As I write this, America is still reeling from its ten-year war in Iraq. The war in Iraq was not a war I supported back in 2001 when the drums of war started being pounded in Washington. One of the many reasons we lingered so long in Iraq is that we had no idea what the cultural impact of such an invasion would be. We "reasoned" that we could bring democracy to Iraq, a country steeped in theocratic rule. What were we thinking? Were we thinking at all? If we had taken the time and care to realize the best way to engender the support of the Iraqi people (after all, it was America who put Saddam Hussein in place to begin with), and to find, perhaps, some other way to help them oust their despotic leader, we might be in a much different place today.

If we grew up in America as Protestants or Catholics of European descent, we are at a disadvantage when it comes to reading the Bible right off the

---

[38] Levine, Amy-Jill (2006). The Misunderstood Jew: The Church and the Scandal of the Jewish Jesus. Harper, p. 53

bat. Jesus was a Jew, and to understand what he said we need to understand a bit about what that means. Jesus grew up in a Jewish village; in fact, more than likely exclusively Jewish.

> *Thus Jesus was socialized into a Jewish social world. Its vision of life was very different from the domination system of Rome and its native collaborators. It was constituted by the sacred traditions of Judaism: its scriptures and stories, worship and festivals, prayers and practices, observances and conventions. Its foundations were practice, the Jewish Bible, and the temple in Jerusalem.*[39]

To translate Jesus from his world into ours is not an easy task, and something I am admittedly not well-equipped to do. Still, in order to move forward into the rest of this book, I must make an attempt, no matter how feeble. I suppose we would have been better off in some way to have been reformed Jews rather than Christians. In other words, Christianity as a religion may not have been the best possible outcome of the vision of a first century Jewish mystic. But we are here, and must begin from where we are. The important thing is that Christianity now begins to re-form itself toward compliance with the vision of that first century Jewish mystic. If not, it runs the risk, I fear, of dying off altogether. The Church is a mere relic in European culture,[40] and here in America it is on the decline.

> *The most rapidly growing religious category today is composed of those Americans who say they have no religious affiliation. While middle-aged and older Americans continue to embrace organized religion, rapidly increasing numbers of young people are rejecting it.*

---

[39] Borg, p. 95

[40] MacCulloch, Diamaid (2009). Christianity: The First Three Thousand Years. Viking, p. 1016

As recently as 1990, all but 7% of Americans claimed a religious affiliation, a figure that had held constant for decades. Today, 17% of Americans say they have no religion, and these new "nones" are very heavily concentrated among Americans who have come of age since 1990. Between 25% and 30% of twentysomethings today say they have no religious affiliation—roughly four times higher than in any previous generation . . . So if more than one-quarter of today's young people are setting off in adult life with no religious identification, compared with about one-20th of previous generations, the prospects for religious observance in the coming decades are substantially diminished.[41]

I see this in my own congregation. The younger a person is, the less likely they are to be at worship services on a regular basis, beginning with my generation (born 1957) and exhibiting this phenomenon exponentially with each ensuing generation. The question is, 'What will be compelling enough to inspire people of these generations, and the generations to come, to pay attention to a first century Jewish mystic from the region of Galilee?' Maybe that's the thing, doing as people did in the first century; compelling people to pay attention to Jesus rather than join a religious organization. When it comes to worship attendance, I tell people to "come and see," just as Phillip told Nathanael.

The next day Jesus decided to go to Galilee. When he got there, he ran across Philip and said, "Come, follow me." (Philip's hometown was Bethsaida, the same as Andrew and Peter.)

---

[41] Putnam, Robert D. and Campbell, David E. (2010). Walking away from church. Los Angeles Times, October 27, 2010.

Philip went and found Nathanael and told him, "We've found the One Moses wrote of in the Law, the One preached by the prophets. It's Jesus, Joseph's son, the one from Nazareth!" Nathanael said, "Nazareth? You've got to be kidding."

But Philip said, "Come, see for yourself." (John 1:43-46).

When we get to know this Jewish mystic, this Jesus, we have something worth inviting people to. We can say, "There's this guy I met, and he says the most amazing things. You really need to hear him for yourself. You've probably heard the name Jesus bandied about, but I'm telling you, until you hear the guy directly—his mouth to your ears—you really haven't heard anything worth hearing. He's the real deal." We will do well to get to know him, and to understand him on his terms, not ours. We will do well to let ourselves be taught by him, not just by the religious leaders who run our institutions. We will do well to work at stripping away all of the religious veneer that keeps us from hearing, really hearing, what Jesus has to say. Then, when we have steeped ourselves in Jesus, we will have something compelling to invite others into.

Several months before I accepted the call to serve the congregation I am currently serving as pastor, (a church named Nazareth, by the way), I read Eugene Peterson's book titled Eat This Book: A Conversation in the Art of Spiritual Reading. In it he lifts up an ancient practice traditionally referred to as lectio divina *(divine reading)*. He takes his title from a passage in revelation.

The voice out of Heaven spoke to me again: "Go, take the book held open in the hand of the Angel astride sea and earth." I went up to the Angel and said, "Give me the little book." He said, "Take it, then eat it. It will taste sweet like honey, but turn sour in your stomach." I took the little book from the Angel's hand and it was sweet honey in my mouth, but when I swallowed, my stomach curdled. (Revelation 10:8-10).

When I arrived at my new call, I was determined to set a precedent that the foundation for Christian community lay in this process. I began a few small groups I decided to call *Scrumptious Scriptures.* In those groups we use a simple process of reading a text, listening to it in silence and then reflecting on how it impacts our lives. I use Jesus texts exclusively. In less than three years, over fifty members of my small town congregation have experienced this means of encountering Jesus in his own words, and many of them have been altered in a very positive way through this process. One woman even attributes this practice of Scrumptious Scriptures as being the catalyst for energizing her to start a food pantry in our church. No board or committee asked her to do this. Somehow she heard the call of Jesus directly, and I have no doubt that since it originates with his call, it will go well.

Another pastor asked me about Scrumptious Scriptures. He asked, "If people just read the text and you do not teach them, how will they interpret it?" It is true; sometimes I do insert some background information about Jesus' world, about the context into which he offered his commentary; but I never tell anyone what it should mean for them. Each one must discover for herself what the words of Jesus mean in her own life. Jesus told parables and then said those who have the capacity to hear what he is saying will hear it; and those who don't, won't. (Matthew 13, Mark 4, Luke 14). My wife says things to me, but I don't always have the capacity to hear what she is saying. Sometimes I have to concentrate, really concentrate in order to get it (and I am better off for doing so). If we are to hear what Jesus is saying, really hear him, then we will need to take the time to concentrate. This process affords us the kind of attentiveness that will be necessary if we are ever going to be transformed by our encounter with a first century Jewish mystic named Jesus.

As Borg reminds us in the quote earlier, Jesus was raised in Nazareth on three basic elements; his Jewish practice, the Jewish Bible, and the temple in Jerusalem. Borg goes into detail about each of these in his book, and I borrow here from him. As for religious practice, Jesus grew up in a theistic culture. There was no separation of church and state for Jesus. All was one and the same. We have seen, for instance, the calls to Muslim prayer (*Salat*) in the world we have entered more deeply since going to war. There is a chant, a call to prayer (*Azaan*) that emanates from loudspeakers throughout the city or town and Muslims stop whatever it is they are doing, fall to their knees, and give homage to Mecca, the birthplace of Muhammad, saying "*Allahu Akbar*" (God is Great). Then a Muslim recites Sura 1 in Arabic, a prayer that begins the day and means in English:

> *In the name of GOD, Most Gracious, Most Merciful;*
> *Praise be to GOD, Lord of the universe.*
> *Most Gracious, Most Merciful; Master of the Day of Judgment;*
> *You alone we worship; You alone we ask for help.*
> *Guide us in the right path, the path of those whom You blessed;*
> *not of those who have deserved wrath, nor of the strayers.*

In the same way Jesus awoke every day to his morning prayer, and went to bed each night with the same prayer, the *Shema*, although there were no loudspeakers.

Attention, Israel!

God, our God! God the one and only!

Love God, your God, with your whole heart: love him with all that's in you, love him with all you've got! (Deuteronomy 6:4-5).

This is followed in Deuteronomy by the mandate to:

Write these commandments that I've given you today on your hearts. Get them inside of you and then get them inside your children. Talk about them wherever you are, sitting at home or walking in the street; talk about them from the time you get up in the morning to when you fall into bed at night. Tie them on your hands and foreheads as a reminder; inscribe them on the doorposts of your homes and on your city gates. (Deuteronomy 6:6-9).

As Jesus grew older he definitely took this mandate literally, for he did indeed "talk about them wherever (he was), sitting . . . or walking in the streets . . . from the time (he) got up in the morning to when (he fell) into bed at night." They got inside of him, were a part of him. This internalization of God's efforts to speak to us is echoed in Jeremiah.

This is the brand-new covenant that I will make with Israel when the time comes. I will put my law within them—write it on their hearts!—and be their God. And they will be my people. They will no longer go around setting up schools to teach each other about God. They'll know me firsthand, the dull and the bright, the smart and the slow. I'll wipe the slate clean for each of them. I'll forget they ever sinned!" God's Decree. (Jeremiah 31:33-34).

The old covenant was literally "cut," animals literally cut up on bloody altars. The old covenant was cut, literally, on the male genitals of its constituents. The old covenant was externally manipulated. But the new covenant will not be so. It will be internalized; it will become a part of one's DNA. It will be so that someone will no longer be able to live one way and believe another. One's faith and one's everyday life will have a symbiotic relationship, and will be indistinguishable one from the other; which leads to a Jesus who is reflected in the later thoughts of John's Gnostic community:

> Then Jesus turned to the Jews who had claimed to believe in him. "If you stick with this, living out what I tell you, you are my disciples for sure. Then you will experience for yourselves the truth, and the truth will free you." Surprised, they said, "But we're descendants of Abraham. We've never been slaves to anyone. How can you say, 'The truth will free you'?"

> Jesus said, "I tell you most solemnly that anyone who chooses a life of sin is trapped in a dead-end life and is, in fact, a slave. A slave is a transient, who can't come and go at will. The Son, though, has an established position, the run of the house. So if the Son sets you free, you are free through and through. I know you are Abraham's descendants. But I also know that you are trying to kill me because my message hasn't yet penetrated your thick skulls. I'm talking about things I have seen while keeping company with the Father, and you just go on doing what you have heard from your father." They were indignant. "Our father is Abraham!"

> Jesus said, "If you were Abraham's children, you would have been doing the things Abraham did. And yet here you are trying to kill

me, a man who has spoken to you the truth he got straight from God! Abraham never did that sort of thing. You persist in repeating the works of your father." They said, "We're not bastards. We have a legitimate father: the one and only God."

"If God were your father," said Jesus, "you would love me, for I came from God and arrived here. I didn't come on my own. He sent me. Why can't you understand one word I say? Here's why: You can't handle it. You're from your father, the Devil, and all you want to do is please him. He was a killer from the very start. He couldn't stand the truth because there wasn't a shred of truth in him. When the Liar speaks, he makes it up out of his lying nature and fills the world with lies. I arrive on the scene, tell you the plain truth, and you refuse to have a thing to do with me. Can any one of you convict me of a single misleading word, a single sinful act? But if I'm telling the truth, why don't you believe me? Anyone on God's side listens to God's words. This is why you're not listening—because you're not on God's side." (John 8:31-47).

Jesus is speaking to Jews, here; likely some prominent Jews who were still living according to externals. Jesus asks, basically, "Who are you listening to? What is inside of you?" It's sort of like a Gatorade commercial that ran a few years ago that asked, "Have you got it in you?" Notice the subtle interplay here between "Father" and "father." There are three fathers represented in this text: **The Father**, the one true God, the God of Jesus' morning and evening prayer, (*Attention, Israel! God, our God! God the one and only! Love God, your God, with your whole heart: love him with all that's in you, love him with all you've got!*); **father Abraham**, the father of religious tradition; and **a father** who is more anti-God, the Devil. Jesus declares here that he listens to *The Father*, and suggests that this Father is not the father these Jewish folks have been listening to. He is speaking from his Jewish tradition, and speaking as a Jew, although John's gospel gets tagged as a very anti-Jewish work.[42]

I think that if Jesus had an encounter like this, and I do not doubt that he did, it was because he took his Jewish upbringing seriously, took the words of the *Shema* seriously, took the words of the prophet Jeremiah seriously, and now asked his followers to take *his* words seriously as well. He is asking his followers to "live out" what he tells them, and promises that in so doing they will *experience* the truth and find real freedom. The truth is not to be known or understood, like some intellectual exercise. The truth is to be experienced in one's everyday living; experienced in the reality of existence. We are to love God with everything we've got, according to the *Shema*. I say to anyone who claims to be Christian, we are to follow Jesus with everything we've got. This begins with the infiltration of everything he has given us; his life, his teachings, his words, and his willingness to risk it all in order to get his point across.

Jesus went to synagogue on Saturdays, in the same way, I suppose, that a growing Christian minority still goes to church on Sundays. Synagogue was a place for worship and prayer, but also a place for social interaction and probably even some community related activities. There were festivals like Passover, Pentecost, the feast of the Tabernacles, and of course, Hanukkah. All of these festivals were meant to be reminders of God's grace and faithfulness to Israel. Keeping traditions and festivals was a part of Jesus' life even as it is still a part of the lives of those who attend a synagogue on a Saturday today, who walk into a Christian church on Sunday today, or who gather any day of the week in a Mosque for prayer

---

[42]   Levine, pp. 102-103

and study of the Qur'an today; even near Ground Zero. To follow Jesus without a willingness to practice is like sitting on your couch claiming that you are jogging because you are watching a video of someone else jogging on your television; or saying how much you love to listen to the music playing on your CD player without hooking up any speakers or headphones—you won't hear any music!

Jesus' words, the words of *The Word*, are essential to any practice; so we must listen to them, avail ourselves of them, and let them get inside of us. This is one of the things our Bibles are for. Jesus' "Bible" was, as stated earlier, divided into three parts: the Torah, the Prophets, and the Writings. He took these writings to heart; let them get inside of him. So when he starts teaching, roaming the countryside, he already has them in him. He knows them and takes them seriously. The passing on of these writings was more oral than written in Jesus' day, especially among the less educated, peasant classes. People did not have "Bibles" like we do today. Written versions of scripture were limited to hand produced scrolls usually kept in synagogues and read publicly on Saturdays. Jesus was often referred to as rabbi, which means teacher, because he quoted freely from these three major bodies of Jewish literature.[43]

In the remaining chapters I will focus on one particular piece of Jesus' teachings, a section from Matthew's version of the Sermon on the Mount. In this section of Matthew Jesus not only iterates from his traditional Jewish scriptural material ("You're familiar with the old written law," Matthew 5:43), but re-iterates that same material in his own words ("I'm telling you . . . I'm challenging that," Matthew 5:21, 44). Jesus gets away from the common penchant to quote scripture as a way of defending one's

-----

[43]   Borg, p. 98

behavior, or one's political position, or one's social status, and ups the ante on the whole deal. One cannot hear these words without wincing a little bit, so be warned. If you have guts to proceed you will hopefully be rewarded, but Jesus did not get crucified for nothing. What you are about to hear may have contributed to his demise. Proceed with caution.

Chapter Four

GIVE ME THAT OLD TIME MURDER

"You're familiar with the command to the ancients, 'Do not murder.' I'm telling you that anyone who is so much as angry with a brother or sister is guilty of murder. Carelessly call a brother 'idiot!' and you just might find yourself hauled into court. Thoughtlessly yell 'stupid!' at a sister and you are on the brink of hellfire. The simple moral fact is that words kill.

"This is how I want you to conduct yourself in these matters. If you enter your place of worship and, about to make an offering, you suddenly remember a grudge a friend has against you, abandon your offering, leave immediately, go to this friend and make things right. Then and only then, come back and work things out with God.

"Or say you're out on the street and an old enemy accosts you. Don't lose a minute. Make the first move; make things right with him. After all, if you leave the first move to him, knowing his track record, you're likely to end up in court, maybe even jail. If that happens, you won't get out without a stiff fine. (Matthew 5:21-26).

For those of you who are counting, or who were raised in the church and sent to catechism class, this is number five of the Big Ten, "Thou Shalt Not Kill!" However, even children who do not go to catechism class or never set foot in a church or a synagogue somehow intuitively know that life is sacred. We all know, with a few psychotic exceptions, not to go around randomly killing people. So we do not probably need commandment number five, really, to get that. We just somehow innately know this.

Oh there are still murders, and the United States is fairly good at it. The U.S.A. ranks 24th out of 62 ranked countries in terms of murder rates.[44] That's nearly the top 3rd of all the countries ranked! Come on, who doesn't love a good murder mystery? Criminal novels, TV shows and films are among the most visited of artistic output. I love them myself, keeping you in suspense until you turn the last page, or watch the last commercial, if they're any good. And if you think it has gotten worse, think again. The homicide rate in the U.S. is about the same today as it was in 1960.[45] So really, very few of us, and probably none of you who are reading this right now, have ever committed a homicide.

What I'm getting at is that commandment number five is relatively easy to keep. Most of us go through our whole lives without ever actually killing someone. In fact, we are better on the whole at not killing than we are at killing, which is strangely comforting, don't you think? If you read your B-I-B-L-E literally, then you can feel pretty good about yourself right about now; pretty smug, even; self-confident. "Hey, I'm not a murderer. I feel great! And what do you know, God thinks I'm swell! But wait; what's that, Jesus? Oh, you mean there's more? You mean I'm not done with this commandment? Gee whiz!"

---

[44] Seventh United Nations Survey of Crime Trends and Operations of Criminal Justice Systems, covering the period 1998-2000 (United Nations Office on Drugs and Crime, Centre for International Crime Prevention).

[45] SOURCES: US Bureau of Justice Statistics (2004), Federal Bureau of Investigation, (2009).

Jesus says we break this commandment just by getting angry, by calling someone an "idiot" or "stupid." Now, how many of us haven't done that? I know I have—lots. I've even called myself an idiot—openly admitted as much to other people. In fact, I'm more likely to call myself an idiot than I am someone else. Does that mean every time I call myself "stupid" I'm committing suicide? Jesus is bordering on absurdity, here, don't you think? Is he serious about this? I say, yes he is. Oh, we can justify this, and brush it off as hyperbole. We can say, "Jesus is just exaggerating to make a point." I think not.

> . . . *Jesus proceeds to interpret the most basic law beginning with the injunction against the first sin of the human race—murder: You must not kill! Obviously we must not kill any other human being, but that is not enough—we must not hate, bear resentment, rage, act in anger against another. We must not insult or humiliate others . . . We must not even appear before God severed from anyone, ready to kill anyone or harm another, even thinking of revenge or getting even with others.*[46]

Already we begin to see how following Jesus is going to be really, really difficult; and why biblical literalism and legalism is so much easier than trying to actually live like Jesus lived. Biblical literalism takes us out of the moment we are in and objectifies life. If we are going to read Jesus we must learn to live with Jesus in every present moment of our lives.

> *Jesus prevents us from thinking that life is a matter of ideas to ponder or concepts to discuss . . . Jesus enables us to take seriously who we are and where we are . . . so that we needn't be someone*

---

[46]   McKenna, Megan (2002) Matthew: The Book of Mercy. New City Press, p. 65

> *else or somewhere else. Jesus keeps our feet on the ground, attentive*
> *to children, in conversation with ordinary people, sharing meals*
> *with friends and strangers, listening to the wind, observing the*
> *wildflowers, touching the sick and the wounded, praying simply*
> *and unselfconsciously . . . Jesus is God here and now.*[47]

We cannot unpack all of this without forcing ourselves to reflect upon relationships. We cannot simply walk around and think ourselves "ok" without assessing our track record with other people. I cannot even begin to tell you how many times in my life I have apologized or asked for forgiveness. It is just a normal part of my life. Self-awareness is a required skill if we are going to follow Jesus. We need to do whatever we need to do in order to acquire some self-awareness; even commandeering professional help, if necessary.

This is a Jesus teaching that is about reconciliation. In a way, they all are. Jesus encourages his listeners, his followers, to "make things right" before even thinking about worshiping God; and one begins to wonder if the making right is not in and of itself the worship. Jesus encourages his followers to even use this approach with their enemies. (I will talk more about enemies in chapter nine). This made me recall something I heard Jon Stewart say once when he was interviewing President Jimmy Carter on The Daily Show; that Carter managed to get through four years of U.S. presidency without dropping one bomb, or invading one country.[48] He reluctantly engaged in military action to address the Iran hostage situation, a military action that failed. Carter was undoubtedly one of the

---

[47] Peterson, Eugene H. (2005). Christ Plays in Ten Thousand Places: A Conversation in Spiritual Theology. William B. Eerdmans, pp. 33-34

[48] Based on my recollection of something Stewart said in his interview with Jimmy Carter October 20, 2010. I was unable to find a transcript.

least hawkish presidents in American history, one of the reasons he was a one term president, perhaps. Instead of military intervention he worked very hard, and still works very hard today, for diplomacy and negotiation as means for bringing peace. It seems to me this is a man that takes his faith seriously, and tries to follow Jesus; even attempting to follow Jesus while he was serving as President of the United States.

Mohandas Gandhi emerged in the early 20th century, quoting Jesus and engaging in nonviolent resistance against the violent and powerful British Empire who relentlessly oppressed the people of India and sowed their seeds of injustice without even blinking an eye. It was journalists from other countries, and especially a journalist from America by the name of Webb Miller who broke the story and made Gandhi's nonviolent fight for justice in India international news. Gandhi and the people who followed him sacrificed greatly, even their lives, in order that justice might be brought to their country. Gandhi and his followers showed us that nonviolent resistance and face to face negotiation can work in the long run. However, just when we think God's kingdom has come on earth and have a chance at real peace, another war breaks out. We resort again and again to violence to solve problems. We aren't listening to Jesus who tells us to make peace with our enemies BEFORE our enemy can even think about using violence against us. I suppose we choose war because it is easier than negotiation, and does not require compromise. As long as we keep choosing war we will not be following Jesus; we will not be living according to the Word of God. We cannot have this both ways. We do not know any other way to solve our problems because we do not seek any other way to solve our problems.

Ironically, it was the Church that developed the *Just War Theory*. Saint Augustine and Thomas Aquinas inaugurated this theory prior to the

Reformation.[49] Even the Reformation did not correct this theory that became religious doctrine and has ended up supporting so many battles.

> *Luther's new position amounts to saying: Insurrection, to be sure, is still forbidden to the Christian; but defensive action in protection of the gospel—even if military means be used, and even if these be directed against the emperor—is not to be counted as insurrection. The use of force in such circumstances may be justified, as in the case of a "just war" according to the classic doctrine, if the end is just, the means appropriate, and if all peaceful means of settlement have failed . . . Under such circumstances, the resort to force is justified.[50]*

The key phrase here clearly requires that *all peaceful means of settlement have failed* before entering into armed confrontation. So, is it murder when our soldiers shoot off their weapons in battle if such a criterion has not been met? Are they breaking the fifth commandment if thorough negotiations have not been attempted? This conundrum is not as easy to unpack as it sounds. From Jesus' point of view I would say the soldiers are merely doing the bidding of the more powerful ones who take us to war, and who quite often fail to exhaust *"all peaceful means of settlement."* The left hand simply does what the right hand wants it to do, even if the right hand isn't quite sure what it is doing in the first place. What do we do with our soldiers who are sent to unjust wars? Jesus would have us deal compassionately with them. So when they come home from Iraq and Afghanistan, we who follow Jesus must certainly extend to them the

[49] MacCulloch, p. 602

[50] Luther, M. (1999, c1971). Vol. 47: Luther's works, vol. 47 : The Christian in Society IV (J. J. Pelikan, H. C. Oswald & H. T. Lehmann, Ed.). Luther's Works (Vol. 47, Page 7). Philadelphia: Fortress Press.

same compassion and mercy Jesus would extend to those who have been treated thusly.

I don't think Jesus would subscribe to the *Just War Theory*. Jesus saw Rome at work every day of his adult life, and he did not like what he saw. Their system was what Borg and others refer to as a domination system. You couldn't go anywhere without seeing the Roman guard, sort of like those images we Americans see on the news of Middle Eastern communities peppered with sub-machine-gun-toting soldiers keeping the "peace." In Jesus' day it was swords and spears, but with the same result—the constant reminder that Rome was watching and that the consequence of defying Rome was likely to result in imprisonment or death. Crucifixion was their response of choice when it came to insurrection. Jesus teaches here, *"say you're out on the street and an old enemy accosts you."* I suspect Jesus' followers, the listeners that day, knew exactly who he was talking about. The "old enemy" was everywhere. Jesus recommends nonviolent resistance as a way of dealing with this old enemy.

> *Jesus was . . . among those advocating and practicing active nonviolent resistance to the domination system. Public criticism, then as now, was a form of resistance. Like some of the prophets of the Jewish Bible, he performed symbolic acts that challenged the symbols of power. He seems also to have taught specific strategies of nonviolent resistance. Indeed, his resistance to the way things were and his counter-advocacy of the kingdom of God led to his execution.*[51]

I say quite often, "Jesus didn't get crucified for nothing." What we have in these passages from Matthew is a collection of teachings that represents

---

[51] Borg, p. 229

material that was likely slipped into his Roman file, a file equivalent to files that might be kept by the FBI here in America today. When one chooses to follow Jesus one is signing up for a counter-cultural tour of duty that involves inherent risk. This is another reason why people find it more amenable to believe in the Bible than to follow Jesus. Someone once told me they could do both. I'm not so sure. The Bible at times advocates *for* war and violence. Remember Psalm 149? Jesus never advocates for war and violence—period.

Violence is embedded in our culture. It is not unusual for me to see children hitting each other. When I do, I say something to those children that encourages love and respect. I tell them Jesus would not want us to hit one another. If we had a lower level of tolerance for this kind of allegedly "friendly" violence when our children are children, we might be able to find it more difficult to talk people into going to war as adults. Perhaps that is precisely the point. We develop into a violence-oriented people. Our games and sporting events promote violence. I have been a Green Bay Packer fan all of my life, but the deeper I find myself traveling into reflection upon Jesus' teaching, the more I begin to wonder whether or not the whole American Football thing is just another insensitivity training effort toward violent solutions to social problems.

George Carlin did a great comedy bit about the difference between football and baseball. He likened football to going to war, using military images like "field general" and "aerial assault." In contrast he said that baseball was "pastoral, a sign of new life. I miss George. While his comedy was no-holds-barred and offensive at times, even he had his moments when the truths of Jesus squeaked through his comedy and into the hearts and minds of his audience. [52]

---

[52]   Carlin, George (1998) Brain Droppings. Hyperion.

I cheer at the local high school football games on Friday nights, under the now culturally labeled Friday Night Lights. I cheer, but I have a knot growing ever so slowly in the pit of my stomach that something is a little off. I hear news stories about the potential long-term effects of head injuries on our children who entertain us on those Friday nights, and I wonder whether it is all worth it. What are we teaching our children? I doubt that Jesus ever spent any time at the Roman Coliseum watching the gladiator's battle? We teach our kids to fight, to do battle. We are not very good at reconciliation, at making things right. Bullying is prevalent in our schools, and we turn a blind eye. We shrug our shoulders and say, "It's just kids being kids. It was the same way when I was a kid." We advocate for cruelty rather than call for reconciliation. And, in the spirit of full disclosure let me tell you that I was indeed a victim of bullying in high school. Nothing has changed. Jesus is advocating here for change.

So, if we are to follow Jesus; if we are to listen to the Word and not just read the Bible, then it will affect our daily lives—our play, our work, our school, our foreign policy, our politics, our culture, and relationships with family, neighbors, and community members. It will no longer be enough for us to walk around proud of the fact that we have never been investigated or incarcerated for murder. The call to follow Jesus, to live by The Word of God made flesh, is a call to active, peaceful, nonviolent living, and unrelenting reconciliation with all of humankind; as well as reconciliation with the natural world we have been given the privilege to be a part of. We are doing violence to that world too as we continue our addiction to fossil fuels and pollute our environment. The good news is it's never too late to make it right.

Chapter Five
What Are You Looking At?

"You know the next commandment pretty well, too: 'Don't go to bed with another's spouse.' But don't think you've preserved your virtue simply by staying out of bed. Your heart can be corrupted by lust even quicker than your body. Those leering looks you think nobody notices—they also corrupt.

"Let's not pretend this is easier than it really is. If you want to live a morally pure life, here's what you have to do: You have to blind your right eye the moment you catch it in a lustful leer. You have to choose to live one-eyed or else be dumped on a moral trash pile. And you have to chop off your right hand the moment you notice it raised threateningly. Better a bloody stump than your entire being discarded for good in the dump. (Matthew 5:27-30).

I have to admit right off the bat that if I were to take Jesus' words literally here, I would definitely be eligible for one of those blue and white signs you hang on the mirror in your car allowing you to have a parking spot as close as possible to your favorite store or restaurant. I would be blind in both eyes, and handless. Lust is one of the seven deadly sins compiled in the fourth century by the Roman monk Evagrius Ponticus, and made popular by the epic poet Dante Alighieri in *The Divine Comedy*. In Dante's poem, however, lust is not isolated to merely sexual appetite. It is relegated to appetite in general; *luxuria*, or extravagance.

No doubt, Jesus' teaching here is focused primarily on a man's lust for a woman, like David and Bathsheba, a story Jesus would have known very well (2 Samuel 11). Enough trouble came of this lusting since it also involved a murder. How many times have we seen this story played out on our favorite detective shows? Women were, in Jesus' day, property. You *had* a wife, or wives; just like you *had* cattle or land or servants or stuff. If this is just a commandment about being a faithful spouse, then once again we have a fairly good track record. I know our cultural statistics are a little heftier on this one than on the murder thing. I know human beings are not naturally monogamous, and that makes this difficult. I know all of that. But still one can find folks who have had marriages lasting 50, 60 and even 70 years who will tell you without equivocation that they have been faithful to their spouses the whole time. In other words, it can be done. It is possible to actually keep this commandment.

Of course, Jesus has to once again go and spoil the whole "I have been pretty good with the adultery" thing by taking it off in a whole new direction, by expanding and broadening the meaning of "lust." Biblical literalists and culturally pietistic politicians and preachers beware. You are not going to wiggle out of this one by quoting the Bible. Besides, there are cameras everywhere these days that unabashedly capture you in their lenses all the while saying, "Pardon me, your lust is showing." Remember the *Shema?*

> *Attention, Israel!*
> *God, our God! God the one and only!*
> *Love God, your God, with your whole heart: love him with all*
> *that's in you, love him with all you've got! (Deuteronomy 6:4-5).*

.

x

.

.

It is God we are to love above everything else. This is, after all, the *first* commandment. To love anything else, anything else at all, more than God is not okay in Jesus' book. Jesus even goes so far as to say to his followers,

> *Don't think that I've come to make life cozy. I've come to cut—make a sharp knife-cut between son and father, daughter and mother, bride and mother-in-law—cut through these cozy domestic arrangements and free you for God. Well meaning family members can be your worst enemies. If you prefer father or mother over me, if you prefer son or daughter over me, you don't deserve me. If you don't go all the way with me, through thick and thin, you don't deserve me. If your first concern is to look after yourself, you'll never find yourself. But if you forget about yourself and look to me, you'll find both yourself and me. We are intimately linked in this harvest work. Anyone who accepts what you do accepts me, the One who sent you. Anyone who accepts what I do accepts the Father, who sent me. (Matthew 10: 34-40).*

Jesus sounds more like a drill sergeant at boot camp here than gentle Jesus, meek and mild. What he is doing is echoing the *Shema*, taking it seriously. He is saying to his followers, "Do you love God with everything you've got; with all your heart and your soul and your mind and your strength? Have you got it in you to be my disciples, because being my disciple means eating, sleeping, and breathing the *Shema*?" It is this Jesus who speaks to us in the fifth chapter of Matthew, beckoning us beyond ourselves to a higher calling, if you will. Lust is all about the self, all about feeding the ego needs of our most base instincts. Lust is the child at the store screaming for that toy on the shelf, and having a fit until she gets it. Lust is focusing on the objects of our desires and feeling unsatisfied until we acquire them.

Think about it; our whole society is built around lust. We are made to want what we do not have every single day of our lives. Unless we crawl under a rock, or live off the grid in the wilderness, we can hardly avoid the influence of capitalism that pervades our culture. Everything is new and improved, bigger and better, superior to last year's model. We are geared toward keeping the economy afloat by wanting more and spending more. We are convinced that our lives, our very survival on this planet depends upon being what society has designated us to be—consumers; and from very young on that is what we are taught to be.

> *In a tempting world there are many things which are deliberately designed to excite the desire, books, pictures, plays, even advertisements. The man whom Jesus here condemns is the man who deliberately uses his eyes to stimulate his desires; the man who finds a strange delight in things which awaken the desire for the forbidden thing. To the pure all things are pure. But the man whose heart is defiled can look at any scene and find something in it to titillate and excite the wrong desire.*[53]

And it is men that Jesus is especially addressing here because it was men in his society that had all the power. Still today this is true in oh so many ways, although women have begun to make their way onto an even playing field; enough so, perhaps, that this text no longer applies exclusively to men. Sorry, ladies. It is the fueling of our desire that Jesus is addressing here, letting the desire get inside of us and replace what the *Shema* says we should have inside of us—only the love of God.

---

[53] Barclay, William (1975). The Gospel of Matthew, Volume 1. Westminster Press, p. 147

One night while working on this book at a resort getaway I took the night off from being locked up alone in my condo writing and went down to the on-sight restaurant and lounge for a friendly game of Texas Hold-'em. I figured it might be fun and give me a break. It was a tournament style game, so a single buy-in was all that was required. There was no way it could escalate throughout the night. There were fewer than 20 people there, and it did not seem like they were all there to have fun. The guy next to me scowled at me once when I first sat down and never looked at me again. Even when he won a pot from me I still could not catch his eye, and he still did not smile. The room was quiet and the feeling stiff. My idea of having some fun playing cards was not panning out.

I think it was because of this that I subconsciously threw *all in* early on in the night. It was a stupid play, and an obvious "tell" since I jumped in early with my declaration. I was the first to leave the tables and walk out into the dark and quiet of the fall evening wondering how I was going to spend the rest of it. It had been about an hour and the night was still "young." There is a casino nearby this resort, and as I approached the steps ascending to my condo's front door I stopped. It was like a siren song saying, "Well, that didn't work out the way you thought it would. Maybe you would have better luck just sitting down at a machine and playing the rest of the night." I stood there on the steps as if in suspended animation. I looked up at the stars. It was a beautiful fall evening. It seemed to take forever to pull myself away from the force of that desire that was sparked by going down and playing poker. It seemed innocent enough at the time, and for some it might not be a problem at all. But for me it was like catnip to the cat, that one drink after years of sobriety for the alcoholic, that cigarette for the ex-smoker. Oh, and by the way, I made it up the stairs and remained in my condo for the rest of the night.

Only you can know what it might be for you, the desire that supplants God in your life. For some it will be sexually related addictions. For some it will be chemicals. For others it will be shopping and spending. It could even be compulsive cleaning. There are anonymous groups meeting somewhere every night of the week, one of which addresses the out of control desire you and I are specifically dealing with, or not dealing with. There are even groups and psycho-therapists that specialize in obsessive-compulsive disorders. Whatever it is that distracts us from having our hearts and minds focused on the most important thing, like loving God or following Jesus, needs to be confronted.

> *Millions of people in our culture make decisions for Christ, but there is a dreadful attrition rate. Many claim to have been born again, but the evidence for mature Christian discipleship is slim . . . Religion in our time has been captured by the tourist mindset. Religion is understood as a visit to an attractive site to be made when we have adequate leisure . . . there are two biblical designations for people of faith that are extremely useful . . . (one of those designations being) 'disciple.' 'Disciple' says we are people who spend our lives apprenticed to our master, Jesus Christ. We are in a growing-learning relationship, always. A disciple is a learner, but not in the academic setting of a schoolroom, rather at the work site of a craftsman. We do not acquire information about God but skills in faith.[54]*

Following Jesus is discipleship for the Christian; just as following Buddha is discipleship for the Buddhist, and following Muhammad is discipleship for the Muslim. By using his tradition in these passages from Matthew Jesus channels the God of his heart and soul, the God he calls Father. Jesus

---

[54] Peterson, Eugene H. (2000). A Long Obedience in the Same Direction: Discipleship in an Instant Society. IVP Books, 2nd ed., pp. 16-17

is, like the prophets he learned about as a kid, taking the old covenant and forging a new one. Jesus is the Word of God that re-interprets the words of scripture, the words of his Bible. Disciples must be willing to engage in this kind of re-interpretation. It will not be enough to merely regurgitate the Bible as if the text itself was enough. As we can see here, and in the text we looked at in the last chapter, Jesus is not satisfied with the text as it is; with the Law as it is. We are going further, traveling into new territory away from the comfortable, cozy religious confines of our local churches. Jesus calls us beyond those walls, beyond our traditions, beyond our catechism classes and our Sunday schools, beyond our women's bible studies and our Sunday morning coffee. Jesus wants us to walk right out of the door and into the squeaky discomfort of living at odds with our own lives. Jesus wants us to live in the tension of our own existence. Our desires, our priorities, our choice-making, our culture itself; it is all on the table and open for assessment and evaluation. Nothing is sacred. Nothing is out of bounds. There is no separation between discipleship and politics. There is no separation between discipleship and family. There is no separation between discipleship and work. There is no separation between discipleship and school. There is no separation between discipleship and The Stock Market. It is all in the mix.

What we look at; what we pay attention to; what we "put inside of us;" everything, if it does not direct us toward following Jesus' teachings and living toward the example of his life, is that thing that needs to be exorcized from our lives. So, what are you looking at? If you are like me I look at a lot. I love television and film and music; but I am also starting to gravitate toward wanting to watch and listen to and read things that will facilitate my discipleship, or encourage in me the following of Jesus. How do I know this? I know this from listening to Jesus; from reading his words and teachings, and examining his life. There is no other way that I know of. It may mean cutting some things out of my life, and it may mean introducing some new things into my life. This is the process, and it is life-long.

I have found that as my eye gets more focused on The Word of God made flesh, my eyes and my ears and my mind all begin to see Jesus' teaching through many of the everyday forms of artistic expression I open myself to. I begin to hear Jesus' voice in the voices of the actors; or rather the screenwriter who gave words to the actors who in turn give those words life. I begin to hear Jesus' voice in the lyrics of the songs I listen to. I begin to see Jesus in the lives of people who aren't even followers of Jesus themselves. There truly is such a phenomenon as eyes to see and ears to hear; but not without the life-long discipline of listening to the Spirit of the One who can give us those eyes and ears by giving him our undivided attention. To use the metaphor of Scrumptious Scriptures (lectio divina), we are what we eat.

> *True religion is relationship, not righteousness. It must play out "on earth as it is in heaven." For this we need clarity and self-consciousness about the nature of our relationships and what makes them inauthentic and death-dealing. If a first century Jew can model a new relationship with God for his disciples, then a twentieth century Jew can define the true nature of the sacred as a personal dialogue. The latter's name is Martin Buber, and the church would do well to remember what he said.*[55]

What Buber said, in a nutshell, is that there are two basic relationships between people; "I-Thou" and "I-It."[56] Jesus is clearly opting for the former

---

[55]   Meyers, Robin R. (2009). Saving Jesus from the Church: How to Stop Worshiping Christ and Start Following Jesus. Harper, p. 207

[56]   Buber, Martin I and Thou (1958). trans. Ronald Gregor Smith. New York: Scribner.

here, that we treat all of humankind with respect, and refrain from the objectification that leads to an "I-It" relationship, the kind of relationship Jesus condemns here. If we are to follow Jesus' teaching then every human being on the planet, every human being we encounter must be a "Thou," someone who is created in God's image, someone who has innate value and worth not because of what they can give us, but because they simply *are*. If we go to worship just for what we can "get out of it" we have missed the point. If we are just in relationships with others for our own self-gratification, then we are, in a way, committing a kind of adultery by betraying the sacredness of those relationships. You see, this is much harder, much more complex than just asking who we are sleeping with. That's just too easy; unless of course you *are* sleeping with someone you're not supposed to be sleeping with, which can get quite complicated.

I suppose one could say that this teaching of The Word gets at the core of our being, our pure identity as God's creatures. This teaching moves us away from power games and role playing to the kind of being that is truly sacred.

This commandment is violated by whatever it is that drives anyone to use other people. Lust for money has led us into a recession and forced us to focus on finances. We are breaking this sixth commandment, according to Jesus, when we abuse others for our own selfish gain, to get what we want, to satiate our desires. It will take due diligence on our parts to monitor our motives, almost like thermometers monitor the temperature. We will need to develop a Jesus consciousness that will not allow us to "forget" what he taught. We can never take a vacation from Jesus if we are to be his disciples. The Word is the Word always and everywhere; whereas a Bible can be left on the shelf at home when we are away.

If we just learn to treat each other with respect—and with the value God bestows upon us so graciously—we will inevitably find ourselves living in a better world. I close this chapter with a lyric to a song I wrote, a song that grows from and encourages this kind of respect and recognition of value in all of us. It is titled *The Beauty in You.*

Take me to a place where
I don't have to hide,
where I can confide in you and be,
just be myself and no one else.

Find in me a mirror to your soul
and look inside, and see
that all you have to do is be,
just be yourself and no one else.

Let me see the beauty in you,
bare your soul to me, tell me what is true;
put all your masks away, we've all got a few.
Let me see the beauty in you.

I have nothing else to offer you,
just room to grow and change into what you were meant to be,
just be, yourself and no one else.

Let me see the beauty in you,
bare your soul to me, tell me what is true;
put all your masks away, we've all got a few.
Let me see the beauty in you.

Chapter Six

D-I-V-O-R-C-E

Remember the Scripture that says, 'Whoever divorces his wife, let him do it legally, giving her divorce papers and her legal rights'? Too many of you are using that as a cover for selfishness and whim, pretending to be righteous just because you are 'legal.' Please, no more pretending. If you divorce your wife, you're responsible for making her an adulteress (unless she has already made herself that by sexual promiscuity). And if you marry such a divorced adulteress, you're automatically an adulterer yourself. You can't use legal cover to mask a moral failure. (Matthew 5:31-32).

I am reminded of the words from the chorus to that heart-wrenching song sung heart-wrenchingly by Tammy Wynette. "Our D-I-V-O-R-C-E becomes final today; me and little J-O-E will be goin' away. I love you both and this will be pure H-E-double L for me. Oh, I wish that I could stop this D-I-V-O-R-C-E."[57]

Divorce is just that—painful, hurtful, and heart-wrenching. All of us know someone who has gone through, or is going through divorce. And when there are children involved it is many times more painful. Today our laws seek to make divorce as palatable as possible, but most people still

---

[57] Music and lyrics by Bobby Braddock & Curley Putnam.

recover from divorce—men and women alike. Why does Jesus tackle this subject here? A liberal theological view is that Jesus was a feminist who was lashing out at a male dominated system. Amy-Jill Levine takes issue with this point of view.

> *To claim that Jesus "liberated" women from a repressive Judaism by forbidding divorce and so protecting women's rights is facile, wrong, and bigoted . . . it is about time Jews and Christians stopped bearing false witness against each other's traditions.*[58]

So, to honor Amy-Jill's appeal to respect her Jewish tradition I shall first quote the passage from Deuteronomy wherein Jesus finds material to expand upon.

> *Suppose a man enters into marriage with a woman, but she does not please him because he finds something objectionable about her, and so he writes her a certificate of divorce, puts it in her hand and sends her out of his house; she then leaves his house and goes off to become another man's wife. Then suppose the second man dislikes her, writes her a bill of divorce, puts it in her hand and sends her out of his house (or the second man who married her dies); her first husband, who sent her away, is not permitted to take her again to be his wife after she has been defiled; for that would be abhorrent to the Lord, and you shall not bring guilt on the land that the Lord your God is giving you as a possession. (Deuteronomy 24:1-4).*[59]

---

[58] Levine, p. 143

[59] Translation from Crossley, James G. (2010). The New Testament and Jewish Law: A Guide for the Perplexed. T &T Clark, p. 69

Jesus seems restless about the practice of simply producing legal papers as a catalyst for divorce. The words that stand out to me in the Matthew text are "selfishness and whim." Jesus is doing what we have long ago stopped doing, discouraging casual divorce. I knew a guy once who was having an affair. He would talk to me about his feelings, etc. And I would say, "What about your commitment to your wife and your kids?" We would go back and forth, back and forth; but over time he chose to reinvest himself in his marriage and his family. Kudos to him! We have become far too reluctant to emphasize the "C" word in this culture—Commitment. This will be dealt with in our next chapter. But really, relationships are something we have with real people, who have real problems, and need real love and support. Jesus flat-out calls breaking relational commitment here a "moral failure."

We tiptoe lightly around this subject because we know so many people who are divorced; and we do not always know *why* they are divorced. In the church divorce used to be less acceptable than it is now. Jesus is in no way denying that there is a legitimate tradition of divorce in Jewish Law. What he is suggesting is that we *stretch* the Law to discourage divorce for any other reasons than absolute necessity. We know that sometimes divorce is something we have to entertain, because to stay married would cause irreparable damage to one or both of the spouses. We know that if one spouse is dysfunctional or abusive, the other spouse sometimes has to leave the marriage; and when this dysfunction or abuse extends to children . . . the sooner the better. This is not what Jesus is talking about here. Jesus is talking about the kind of divorce that is based on, "I'm not happy with this one; I'll try that one." Relationships require more respect than this.

I realize that I am opening myself up to some potential flack. When we took on this whole passage from Matthew 5 at *Scrumptious Scriptures* this is the section that was the hardest for the group to digest. The Living Word of God does not agree with our current divorce practices, much less the divorce practices of his own day. The Law was not the problem; it was the way the Law was used. In the Bible we can find agreement and justification for our divorce practices, but not with the Word of God. He simply will not comply with what makes us comfortable and cozy; and the desire to be comfortable and cozy may very well be the reason people marry now to begin with.

Alison Clarke-Stewart and Cornelia Brentano, both professors of psychology at California universities, shed light on this idea that personal happiness and satisfaction have become primary motivational factors for marriage in our time.

> ... *the primary purpose of marriage today seems to be the satisfaction of personal needs for affection and moral support. Several observers have suggested that a decline in commitment to marriage as a bond for life may be contributing to the high level of divorce. It appears that the primary motivation for marriage is personal happiness. A greater emphasis is now placed on mutual feelings of love and fulfillment than on obligation to marriage vows and children, and marriages are supposed to be based on romantic love and free choice, not duty and dynasty.*[60]

Commitment to marriage and the desires of the Ego seem to be a potent cocktail that can cause explosive results. Ms. Stewart suggests this is a new trend, but it seems from Jesus' inference here that the trend began a long, long time ago. It is only now, in our current "me first" society that we have

---

[60] Clarke-Stewart, Alison (2007). Divorce: Causes and Consequences: Current Perspectives in Psychology. Yale University Press, p. 31

propped up this trend as almost fashionable through best-selling self-help psychology books and trashy grocery store rags that elucidate how our pop idols flip-flop from one marriage to another, further undergirding the notion that marriage is all about the flavor of the month rather than a commitment for life. Celebrities go on talk shows and are applauded for sustaining a long-term marriage in Hollywood, as if this is the exception; which it may very well be. Jesus' teaching is perhaps more relevant today than it was in his day. He has been speaking for 2,000 years and we still don't seem to be listening.

Some might say that monogamy is the issue, that we are not naturally monogamous. We have somehow come to these conclusions, I suppose, by elevating our promiscuity to a position above our ability to make and keep commitments. We may not be "naturally" monogamous, but we have the capacity to be monogamous. I may not "naturally" feel like exercising, but I have the capacity to exercise. I may not "naturally" want to floss my teeth, but I have the capacity to floss my teeth. I may not "naturally" love the unlovable, but I have the capacity to love the unlovable; and doing so is part of the call to follow Jesus (see chapter nine). Making a commitment to love someone is different from "feeling like" loving someone.

I don't think God always "feels like" loving humankind. We do some pretty terrible stuff. Still, day after day, in a church or a synagogue somewhere, a preacher or teacher declares God's undying love for humankind; God's relentless, unconditional, unfailing love. I believe in a God who loves like this because without a "higher power" to lean on I may very well never be able to come close to loving like this. Long-term marriage commitment requires this kind of relentless, unconditional, unfailing love. So, like any member of an anonymous group I begin and end my day with the undeniable declaration that I cannot do it on my own; that I do indeed need a "higher power" if I am going to follow Jesus and let the Word of God live inside of me.

Judaism and Christianity and Islam are all monotheistic religions. I suppose one could argue that at the very foundation of these religions lays the core concept of monogamy—One God, One People. But this is not reason enough to advocate for commitment in marriage. The love of God is nothing if it is not experienced in real time, through real people. When I love my spouse unconditionally, and she loves me without exception, we are offering one another the greatest of gift—the incarnation of God's love in real life. The Word of God became flesh and lived among humankind. When we commit ourselves in relationship to the extent that we are capable of in marriage, we have the opportunity to re-incarnate the Word of God. The Word of God will not be, then, merely ink on paper bound in a book on a shelf in the house somewhere, but an actual living, breathing Word—the Word of God.

Jesus is not just engaging in social commentary. Jesus is not just lobbying to be invited on the Oprah Winfrey Show to promote some sort of self-help book on marriage. His goal is, I think, to have marriage, and all of our relationships really, be opportunities to put real flesh and blood on the Word of God; to embody in real life the life God intends for us, and has intended for us from the beginning. Jesus sees marriage as part of the big picture, and wants us to do the same. To make it any less is to deny the power and potency of the Word. To diminish the value of marriage is to destroy the very thrust of God's unconditional, unfailing, relentless love into the world. The commitments we make to each other, more often than not in the presence of God in a church, synagogue or mosque, are sacred commitments. Wouldn't it be best for us to treat them as such?

Which brings me to what, I believe, must be a part of this conversation. Marriage is undoubtedly beholden to the social "norms" and customs of its time and location both in history and in the world. Throughout history, and from one country (even one region) to another, customs, laws, traditions, and views of marriage vary greatly. I am not an anthropologist and will not debate here the pros and cons of any marriage practice. What I will do, however, is to suggest that since the Word of God confronts "selfishness and whim" in this text as these tendencies impose themselves upon committed relationships, we need to evaluate our religious and cultural dialogue about people who are in "different" relationships. Insofar as we have human beings that long to be in committed long-term relationships, who want to love each other as God does—unconditionally; and who want to witness to the amazing love of the Word made flesh through their relationships, I say, "What is the problem?" And don't tell me, "The Bible says," because the Bible is just a pile of paper and ink. The Bible doesn't speak. The only Word I am interested in hearing is a Living Word. Does Jesus have anything to say about this? It would certainly be interesting to have him with us as we go through this time of cultural upheaval. The only path for us is to listen to Jesus, listen to his words and teachings, and observe his life before we go off quoting the Bible to each other.

Talk about divorce! I have seen my denomination, the Evangelical Lutheran Church in America torn apart because of one issue—the willingness to let openly same-sexed human beings in committed monogamous relationships serve according to God's call as pastors in the church. Over 400 ELCA congregations in the United States have been torn apart, ripped in two in many cases, because our commitment to one another in the church cannot somehow withstand this disagreement. I know a couple in my own congregation that is split right down the middle on this issue. As far as I know, they are not filing for divorce papers because they cannot agree about same-sex relationships. If marriages can stay together even if spouse disagrees with spouse on this matter, why can't congregations? Do we have to "split up" every time we disagree over a controversial issue?

The landscape of Christianity is peppered with so many denominations, groups and sects that I doubt we can even keep an accurate count. Christians are perhaps the most divided and divisive religious bunch on the planet. Any time we disagree we run off, find people we can agree with, and start another group. I don't know about you, but this sounds strangely similar to that divorce stimulant, "I'm not happy with this one; I'll try that one." Perhaps our divorce practices, and our cultural penchant for individual pleasuring, have fueled the fire for this divisiveness and dissension in the church. If we cannot stay committed to one person, how are we going to stay committed to a whole bunch of people?

> *Sectarianism involves deliberately and willingly leaving the large community . . . and embarking on a path of special interests with some others . . . who share similar tastes and concerns . . . We wouldn't put up with an art dealer cutting up a large Rembrandt canvas into two-inch squares and selling them off nicely framed. So why do we so often positively delight and celebrate the dividing up of the Jesus community into contentious and competitive groups? And why does Paul's rhetorical question, "Has Christ been divided?" (1 Cor. 1:13), continue to be ignored century after century?*[61]

I think Jesus is speaking to this very issue in Matthew, although he had no idea at the time what a big mess we would make in his name. Yes, we have done this in his name, in the name of the Word of God. What I have

---

[61]   Peterson, Eugene H. (2005). *Christ Plays in Ten Thousand Places: A Conversation in Spiritual Theology.* William B. Eerdmans, pp. 239-240.

71

seen in the last few years saddens me deeply. The pain that this behavior has brought into the lives of clergy and laity alike is no different from the pain inflicted by divorce. It is the pain that comes from witnessing other human beings at their worst. It is the pain that is born from hatred and resentment, vitriol and spite. These are not behaviors and emotions I relate to followers of the Word. These are behaviors that come from the core of our Egos, and they are not the best of who we are, or who God created us to be.

> *The impulse to sectarianism has its roots in "selfism," the conceit that I don't need others as they are but only for what they can do for me . . . Sects are composed of men and women who reinforce their basic selfism by banding together with others who are pursuing similar brands of selfism, liking the same foods, believing in the same idols, playing the same games, despising the same outsiders.*[62]

"Selfism" is Peterson's word, but I think a good one to sum up what the Word is getting at in Matthew 5:31-32. If there is any sin to be confronted it is not people's reactions to same-sex relationships, or even casual divorce, but rather the "selfism" that underlies them both. My denomination is suffering mostly from "selfism" right now, and the D-I-V-O-R-C-E that plagues her. What we need to do is take the Word with us as we sniff out anything we might be using to support our "selfism" in the Bible. This is one way the Word can best be used to "interpret" the Bible. For me to read the Bible without first "consulting" the Word is dangerous and can be detrimental to my health, and to the health of others. The Word of God makes the Bible a tool for discerning how best to reach out to others and make the world a better place for everyone to live. We could try that.

---

[62]   Peterson, Eugene H. (2005). *Christ Plays in Ten Thousand Places: A Conversation in Spiritual Theology.* William B. Eerdmans, pp. 241-242

It might be a good idea. Jesus' prayer in John's gospel calls us to oneness, and to love. Hear then The Word of God praying for you, and for me; and remember that we are the answer to His prayer.

> The goal is for all of them to become one heart and mind—
>> Just as you, Father, are in me and I in you,
>> So they might be one heart and mind with us.
>> Then the world might believe that you, in fact, sent me.
>> The same glory you gave me, I gave them,
>> So they'll be as unified and together as we are—
>> I in them and you in me.
>> Then they'll be mature in this oneness,
>> And give the godless world evidence
>> That you've sent me and loved them
>> In the same way you've loved me.

>> Father, I want those you gave me
>> To be with me, right where I am,
>> So they can see my glory, the splendor you gave me,
>> Having loved me
>> Long before there ever was a world.
>> Righteous Father, the world has never known you,
>> But I have known you, and these disciples know
>> That you sent me on this mission.
>> I have made your very being known to them—
>> Who you are and what you do—
>> And continue to make it known,
>> So that your love for me
>> Might be in them
>> Exactly as I am in them. (John 17:21-26).

Chapter Seven

PROMISES, PROMISES

And don't say anything you don't mean. This counsel is embedded deep in our traditions. You only make things worse when you lay down a smoke screen of pious talk, saying, 'I'll pray for you,' and never doing it, or saying, 'God be with you,' and not meaning it. You don't make your words true by embellishing them with religious lace. In making your speech sound more religious, it becomes less true. Just say 'yes' and 'no.' When you manipulate words to get your own way, you go wrong. (Matthew 5:33-37).

The commitment I am most urging in this book is a commitment to following Jesus. We can be committed, or not committed, to many things; but this is the one most important thing for those who call themselves Christians. However, I understand that Jews, Muslims, Buddhists, Hindus, and others also listen to Jesus and his teachings. This is not an exclusively Christian practice. Here Jesus is taking on yet another commandment, one of the Big Ten. As best I can tell Jesus is now embellishing what looks to be the second commandment.

You shall not take the name of the Lord your God in vain.

I am a Lutheran pastor who happens to have been born and raised in the Lutheran Church; Missouri Synod, Wisconsin Synod, American

Lutheran, and now ELCA. So I have been born and raised to synthesize the commandments through Luther's Small Catechism. Luther wrote simple explanations to each of the commandments in the catechism. His explanation of the second commandment is:

> We should fear and love God, and so[5] we should not use his name to curse, swear,[6] practice magic, lie, or deceive, but in every time of need call upon him, pray to him, praise him, and give him thanks.[63]

This explanation of the commandment sums up well what I have experienced in my traditional learning as a child, and what I think many pastors and catechism teachers still teach regarding this commandment—namely that we should watch what we say. This is not a bad approach. After all, a chunk of the book of James is dedicated to the potential evils of the tongue (James 3:1-12). I remember that scene in the film *A Christmas Story*[64] when Ralphie is helping his dad change a tire. His dad carefully placed the nuts in the hubcap that Ralphie held in his hands. Then, suddenly, his father bumped the cap and the nuts went flying off into the snow. Ralphie uttered, in slow motion, "Oh ffffudge!" The narrator, speaking for Ralphie as he remembers the incident then retorts, "Only I didn't say 'fudge;' I said THE word; the big one; the queen mother of dirty words; the 'F' dash, dash, dash word." The next scene finds Ralphie being confronted by his mother with . . . yes, a bar of soap. Supposedly this is what mothers did back in the fifties, washed their children's mouths out with soap whenever they said a bad word.

---

[63] Tappert, T. G. (2000, c1959). The Book of Concord : The Confessions of the Evangelical Lutheran Church. The Small Catechism: I, 4). Philadelphia: Fortress Press.

[64] The movie *A Christmas Story* is based on Jean Shepherd's *In God We Trust, All Others Pay Cash*, originally published in 1966.

So, Luther's explanation to the second commandment has given mothers and fathers comfort that their children were learning at church what they didn't necessarily learn at home, that certain words were to be understood as taboo. Ralphie's father was the king of dirty words, by the way. My apologies, then, to mothers and fathers everywhere who expect me to jump on that bandwagon. I do not teach that *any* words are "bad" in and of themselves. Words are just tools we use to communicate whatever it is that we happen to want to communicate. I am using words right now. No one word I am using has any more or less moral weight than another. Besides, words are easy. I am writing these words almost as easily as I am breathing in and out as I write them. It is even easier, sometimes, for me to run at the mouth, which can cause a certain degree of damage to those who must endure my verbal diarrhea. No, it is not the words in and of themselves that cause any kind of pain or damage. The words alone have little innate energy, little power. But the *use* of words, the energy underneath the words; now there you've got something worth looking at.

> *A bit in the mouth of a horse controls the whole horse. A small rudder on a huge ship in the hands of a skilled captain sets a course in the face of the strongest winds. A word out of your mouth may seem of no account, but it can accomplish nearly anything—or destroy it! It only takes a spark, remember, to set off a forest fire. A careless or wrongly placed word out of your mouth can do that. By our speech we can ruin the world, turn harmony to chaos, throw mud on a reputation, send the whole world up in smoke and go up in smoke with it, smoke right from the pit of hell. (James 3:3-6)*

Remember, it was words, or rather energy expressed through words, that brought all of creation into existence according to the first creation story in Genesis. When we speak, or write as I am doing here, we create; we exert energy upon the world. If there is anger and vitriol behind our words, then we invoke anger and vitriol, creating an angry and vitriolic world. If there is love and peace behind our words, then we invoke love and peace, creating a more loving and more peaceful world. It is not words that matter, but rather the energy that resides behind, underneath, and within the use of those words. When I speak, or write, what intention resides within whatever it is I am expressing? Is it the "selfism" Peterson referred to in the last chapter, or am I truly focused on others and making the world a better place within which to exist?

The second commandment—*Do not take God's name in vain*—means that we are not to live our lives in servitude to our Egos, but to pour ourselves out selflessly upon the world as Jesus did. Taking God's name, means we are running around calling ourselves God's people. Jesus is saying, "If you are going to call yourselves by God's name then act like you are God's people! Live like it is true. Live like I live!" In the same way I am saying now, if you call yourself a Christian, a Christ person, a Jesus person, "Then act like it! Live like it is true. Live like you are following Jesus! Live like nothing else matters so much as incorporating what he lives and teaches into your life." To do anything less is to take his name, to take the Word, in vain.

It is easy not to say certain words. We can piously tell others, "Oh, I don't swear. I don't like it when people say this word or that word." As a pastor I can't tell you how many times people have corrected themselves because they were with me, a pastor, as if somehow my evaluation of them mattered, and as if I was simply keeping track of the 'bad' words people used. Furthermore, this evokes in us a fickle image of a God who simply marks how many times we use the queen mother of all dirty words instead of a God who is more interested in the degree of our commitments to follow Jesus, or to honor and respect one another. This section from Matthew points in the direction of the latter, calls us to a deeper commitment, a deeper walk with the Word made flesh, with Jesus.

> *If the church is to survive as a place where head and heart are equal partners in faith, then we will need to commit ourselves once again not to the worship of Christ, but to the imitation of Jesus. His invitation was not to believe, but to follow. Since it was once dangerous to be a follower of The Way, the church can rightly assume it will never be on the right track again until the risks associated with being a follower of Jesus outnumber the comforts of being a fan of Christ. Until we experience Jesus as a "radically disturbing presence," instead of a cosmic comforter, we will not experience him as a true disciple.*[65]

It is a disturbing trend that fewer and fewer families seek to follow Jesus as a family. I have a small group of Confirmation students in my congregation. I rarely see their families at worship; not that worship attendance is the only barometer of whether or not we are following Jesus. I think that, if we are intent on following Jesus we will need all of the support we can get, and one of the places we go for support is the church. If the church is at its best, it is a home, an oasis, and a training ground for following Jesus. I realize that the quality of Christian communities varies in this regard, but we must aspire to grow deeper into the One we are called to follow. As congregations grow to understand that they exist to encourage growth in this direction and not just growth for growth's sake, I hope we will discover that people will be drawn to Jesus rather than flashy programs or entertaining worship services.

---

[65] Meyers, p. 145.

Jesus is reinterpreting the second commandment. I am reinterpreting the second commandment based upon Jesus' reinterpretation. This is how I am asking us to read the Bible now, if we are Christians. It will not be enough for us to stop using certain words so that we can smugly pat ourselves on the back for being all moral and righteous. That is too easy. Instead, we will need to evaluate our level of commitment to following Jesus. Are we willing to take the time to listen to his words, to study his life, to let his teachings get inside of us and transform us from the inside out? The people who attend *Scrumptious Scriptures* groups have guts—real guts—because they are risking change. When we read the Word made flesh, we are giving up control; we are letting a "higher power" take over. When we read the Bible through *His* eyes, and with *His* sensibility, we are giving up control. We are no longer looking for justifications to "get our own way." We are, instead, seeking to follow The Way, the Jesus way, the way that I am just beginning to learn how to follow after 27 years of ordained ministry and a half a lifetime in the church.

Jesus used seed imagery (Matthew 13; Mark 4; Luke 8). I think sometimes this effort to follow Jesus is like seeds that are planted. I now serve in a rural area where every year farmers plant their seeds and hope for the best; they plant the seeds in the spring and await the harvest in the fall. Jesus understood this. Jesus knew there was patience involved in planting and harvesting. As I look back over a half a life lived I realize that it has taken all this time for the seed of the Word to grow, and it is nowhere near harvest time. But the planting must take place if the seeds are to have a chance at growing.

When we listen to Jesus, the Word, we are letting Him be planted in us. The process begins with the planting. We cannot go about doing other things and expect the seeds to grow when they have not been planted.

What I am hoping we will do as a result of reading this book is let the seed of the Word, of Jesus, be planted in us, so that our use of His name will not be in vain. The Indian mystic and teacher Osho (1931-1990) taught,

> *Growth is a rare phenomenon. It is natural, yet rare. When the seed has found the right soil, it grows. It is very natural; growth is natural. But to find the right soil—that is the very crux of the matter. (Taken from the discourses of Osho).*

The Word is the seed, and we are the soil. We need communities that work that soil, that nurture that soil, that make that soil conducive to growth. Would that our congregations would grow to become healthy communities, rich soil where we can grow deeper into this Jesus, this Word who longs to become flesh again in and through our lives. We need to stop playing "church" or subscribing to an "ism" (Lutheranism, Catholicism, and Protestantism), and start following Jesus, together; supporting one another on the journey. We need to make commitments that run deeper than our own "selfism," commitments to following Jesus, and commitments to supporting one another as we seek to follow.

> *Whatever else my relationship with Jesus Christ may be, it is not just some ambiguous New Age thing, where I try to get in touch with a self-defined spirit of the universe. There is quite a gulf between biblical Christian spirituality and Star Wars spirituality ("Use the force, Luke"). Star Wars is great entertainment and even all the stuff about "the force" is kind of inspiring, but what about life in the real world? Christians believe that "the force" became flesh and lived among us (compare John 1:14). We believe that "the force" is a person who has a name and a personality, a person who left a historical record regarding what he said and did in this*

world . . . If Jesus really is risen, raised from the dead and living now with a spiritual body, then we can indeed have a relationship with a Jesus who is real, not just imaginary. We can come to know this Jesus and be challenged by him.[66]

We take Jesus' name in vain when Jesus is relegated to a mere talisman we carry around in our pockets to ward off evil spirits, or to dispel weather we find inhospitable to our plans, or to insure some sort of heavenly accommodations when we die, or to make us feel better about the messes we make, or to allow us to feel superior to others; and worst of all to make us "right." The second commandment calls us to unabashed faithfulness to God. In Jesus, God has redefined that faithfulness, identifying it with the path Jesus walks.

Jesus arose out of the river Jordan and a voice was heard saying, "This is my Son, chosen and marked by my love, delight of my life."[67] In Jesus God is saying to the whole world, "I want you to live like this. I want you to be like this. In life of this person, this Jesus, you have the embodiment of what it means to live out *The Shema*. Pay attention to this kid of mine and you will have life—real life."

I remind you also that Jesus is not exclusive in this way. God has sent others to show us the path, and each of us needs to choose who we will follow most closely. There was a scene in that great film *Oh God!*, starring George Burns in the title role. Jerry (played by the late John Denver, the folk-singer) was locked up in a hotel room with a series of questions in Aramaic, the ancient language Jesus spoke, in order to prove to a group of religious leaders whether or not he really had an encounter with God.

---

[66]   Powell, Mark Allan (2004). Loving Jesus. Fortress Press, pp. 28 & 30
[67]   Matthew 3:17

Faithfully, God shows up in his hotel room and answers the questions—sort of. God certainly doesn't give the answers the religious leaders expect.

One question was simply, "Was Jesus the son of God?" Having read the question God (Burns) drops the sheet of paper on the table, shakes his head, and paces a bit. Then he says, "Jesus was my son. Moses was my son. Mohammed was my son. Buddha was my son. And so are you. And so is the guy who's charging you $18.50 for a piece of room service roast beef." God can speak anytime, anywhere, and through anyone God chooses. For us to put limits on God's voice is to narrow our ability to hear that voice. This narrowing is also a "taking in vain." It is important that we choose a path and do the work necessary to follow that path. I have chosen the Jesus path. It is also important that we stay open to the paths that others choose, and open to hearing God speak on those highways and byways as well, using the Word of God as our primary evaluative tool for processing those words spoken by others. This is part of our being answers to Jesus' prayer, and becoming one.

"Selfism" lures us into a false sense of security that comes with sectarianism and denominationalism. These are smoke-screens for the real thing, distractions from the following. When we become so wrapped up in a particular expression of faith that we either discount all others, or worse make war with all others, we literally become the vanity that God is condemning in this commandment. There is one God, and many expressions of God's reality in the world. Jesus happens to be my favorite, the expression I was nurtured in since I was a child, and the one I know best. It makes sense for me to make the choice to follow Jesus. I just wish I had made it sooner.

When we look into and touch deeply the life and teaching of Jesus,
we can penetrate the reality of God. Love, understanding, courage,

and acceptance are expressions of the life of Jesus. God made Himself known to us through Jesus Christ. With the Holy Spirit and the Kingdom of God within him, Jesus touched the people of his time. He talked with prostitutes and tax collectors, and had the courage to do whatever was needed to heal His society. As a child of Mary and Joseph, Jesus is the Son of Woman and Man. As someone animated by the energy of the Holy Spirit, He is the Son of God.[68]

These are the words of a Buddhist, a Buddhist who takes the task of following Jesus more seriously than many Christians; more seriously, perhaps, then *most* Christians. Hahn has not taken what he has taken in vain. He is a devout Buddhist who follows the life and teachings of The Buddha, while also incorporating other great expressions of how God attempts to speak to humankind, not least of all that expression who is Jesus of Nazareth, The Christ. To do any less is to take the name of the Lord our God in vain. To do any less is to violate the second commandment of the Big Ten. To do any less is to spurn *The Shema* Jesus loved and practiced in his own life as a devoted Jew.

When I wrote A Long Obedience twenty years ago, I was a parish pastor writing for my parishioners . . . Two convictions undergirded my pastoral work. The first conviction was that everything in the gospel is livable and that my pastoral task was to get it lived . . . lived in detail, lived on the streets and on the job, lived in the bedrooms and kitchens, lived through cancer and divorce, lived with children and in marriage. Along the way I found that this also meant living it myself, which turned out to be the far more formidable assignment. I realized that this was going to take some

---

[68] Hahn, pp. 35-36

time. I settled in for the long haul . . . The second conviction was
that my primary pastoral work had to do with . . . helping people
listen to God as personally and as honestly as we could in lives of
prayer.[69]

I find myself now, for the first time in over 27 years of parish ministry in the same mode of leadership that Peterson found himself in 30 years ago. Without a solid foundation of listening to the Word of God and opening our hearts to the Word of God we will simply be building our lives on sinking sand, shaky ground; we will be taking God's name in vain. We cannot continue to "play church." We cannot be satisfied to hang a cross around our necks without at the same time realizing that the very cross that hangs there is a cross of our own, a cross that calls us to follow, a cross that interrupts our ordinary, everyday lives and calls us beyond ourselves to a world that is starving for justice, ravenous for peace, hungry for hope, and famished for what only the unconditional love of God can provide.

Those first words of Jesus from this section of Matthew haunt. He says, "And don't say anything you don't mean." There is a popular saying that is like this—"Say what you mean and mean what you say." There is a call herein to be people of The Word; which is not the same as saying we should be people of The Bible, but rather encouraging us to be people who understand that words create reality, and that one very primary expression of God's Word to the world is Jesus. When Jesus' words and life and teachings live in us and become reality, then we are in keeping with this second commandment and in touch with Jesus' re-interpretation of this second commandment. This is what will once again give life to our churches and religious communities; and life to us.

---

[69]   Peterson, A Long Obedience, pp. 201-202

Chapter Eight

An Eye for an Eye Makes the Whole World Blind

"Here's another old saying that deserves a second look: 'Eye for eye, tooth for tooth.' Is that going to get us anywhere? Here's what I propose: 'Don't hit back at all.' If someone strikes you, stand there and take it. If someone drags you into court and sues for the shirt off your back, giftwrap your best coat and make a present of it. And if someone takes unfair advantage of you, use the occasion to practice the servant life. No more tit-for-tat stuff. Live generously. (Matthew 5: 38-42).

On September 11, 2001 the United States of America experienced her version of Pearl Harbor II, the first attack by a foreign entity on American soil in the 21st century. It was a terrible thing watching those towers fall, anxiously waiting for yet another attack somewhere else. We did not know when we turned on our televisions that day if this was it, or if this was just the beginning of a more massive effort. It was a horrible, horrible day. Over 3,000 people died that day. Our airplanes were grounded. American life came to a halt. It was indeed another infamous day for America.

I was on staff in the congregation I served at the time, and it was my turn to preach on the Sunday following. I don't remember what I said that day, but I do remember that I chose to preach about forgiveness. I somehow knew even then that Jesus would respond to such horrors with a forgiving, loving heart. With butterflies in my stomach I talked about the Jesus who loves and forgives even his enemies, and the call for us to do the same. But this was not the popular sentiment in the culture.

> *A day cannot live in infamy without the nourishment of rage. Let's have rage.*

> *What's needed is a unified, unifying, Pearl Harbor sort of purple American fury--a ruthless indignation that doesn't leak away in a week or two, wandering off into Prozac-induced forgetfulness or into the next media sensation (O.J . . . . Elian . . . Chandra . . .) or into a corruptly thoughtful relativism (as has happened in the recent past, when, for example, you might hear someone say, "Terrible what he did, of course, but, you know, the Unabomber does have a point, doesn't he, about modern technology?").*

> *Let America explore the rich reciprocal possibilities of the fatwa. A policy of focused brutality does not come easily to a self-conscious, self-indulgent, contradictory, diverse, humane nation with a short attention span. America needs to relearn a lost discipline, self-confident relentlessness--and to relearn why human nature has equipped us all with a weapon (abhorred in decent peacetime societies) called hatred.[70]*

These words from Lance Morrow in *Time* magazine written just a few days after the fact reflect the mood and spirit of the American people at the time. We wanted retribution. We had hatred in our hearts for the

---

[70] Morrow, Lance (2001). The Case for Rage and Retribution, Time Magazine, September 14, 2001.

people who did this terrible thing; even though it wasn't quite clear who these people were at the time. We had a sneaking suspicion that they were Muslim, a confirmed suspicion that even today causes so many Americans to simply hate the whole enterprise, as if somehow *all* Muslims were poised to drop the big one on our country and destroy our way of life; a lie propagated by certain religious groups and one particular, very powerful news agency. Anti-Islamic sentiment will be an issue in this country for a long time to come, but it is not in keeping with the Word of God.

I preached my sermon and was dressed down by what was soon to be a former member of the congregation immediately following the service. I think it gave the people that day an alternative to the likes of Morrow; an alternative to what they heard when they turned on their televisions again that day. Jesus offers us an alternative to hating and destroying our enemies. He recommends loving our enemies. He suggests non-violent resistance, the kind practiced by Gandhi and King, Jr.; the kind Jesus himself practiced when he stood before his powerful antagonists and took a beating. Jesus practiced what he preached.

But we do not seem to want to do this. I stood outside every Saturday morning through the winter of 2001-2002, through the year 2002, and into the winter of 2002-2003, holding a sign with the sometimes 100 plus other citizens of our community (not much in a town of 10,000), imploring our government, and our fellow citizens, not to react to this atrocity by going to war in yet another country. But the drums of war were already banging away in Washington, D.C., and the bully pulpit of the president was greater than a few ragtag citizens standing on street corners around the country. International protests were also formed. Across the street from us an even smaller group of war veterans gathered to advocate for war. It is what they knew. It is how they had been nurtured to respond to such matters. I understood that, and had compassion for them.

We were already at war in Afghanistan, and still are as I write these words. That war started in October of 2001; we were already reacting to the attacks of September 11th with violence. But the war gods of Washington were not satisfied. They had Iraq in their sights. So we thought maybe, just maybe we could mount a non-violent counter-insurgency Jesus-style. On February 15, 2003 somewhere between 10 and 20 million people took to the streets in about 60 countries world-wide in an effort to deter the impending war in Iraq. But even the volume generated by this non-violent protest fell on deaf ears in Washington, D.C.

On March 20th, 2003 the U.S. military started the war in Iraq with a grand display of military might called 'Operation Shock and Awe' pummeling Baghdad and other primary sites in Iraq with a barrage of air strikes that looked like the Fourth of July on the ground. We watched this on our television sets, some Americans salivating over the fact that we were finally getting those bastards back for what they had done to us, and others of us looking on in horror and thinking about all of the innocent people who would die that night. Nearly 20,000 human beings have died in Afghanistan since we started military operations there in the fall of 2001 and half of those dead are civilians. But in Iraq the story is quite different. In a shorter span of time over 900,000 have died, and over 865,000 of them are civilians.[71]

Over 3,000 people died here in the United States in 2001 as a result of a malicious attack by Muslim extremists driven by forces that are more

---

[71] http://www.unknownnews.net/casualties.html

powerful and diverse than the ones who flew those planes.[72] By the time all is said and done nearly 1,000,000 civilian lives, over 1,600,000 lives including all of the troops involved, will be lost in two countries half-way around the world because we wanted retribution. If we had only listened to Jesus all of these deaths could have been avoided.

Mahatma Gandhi is quoted as having said, "An eye for an eye makes the whole world blind." In the case of our reaction to 9/11, an eye for an eye makes the whole world dead, or at least a significant chunk of it. A million and half people in a world of nearly 7 billion human beings are, from a military point of view, collateral damage. This doctrine of retribution comes from The Bible. Yes, Jesus disagrees with The Bible. Here is what Jesus and other Jewish children were taught growing up in Nazareth and the rest of Galilee.

> *Anyone who takes the life of a human being is to be put to death. Anyone who takes the life of someone's animal must make restitution—life for life. Anyone who injures their neighbor is to be injured in the same manner: fracture for fracture, eye for eye, tooth for tooth. The one who has inflicted the injury must suffer the same injury. Whoever kills an animal must make restitution, but whoever kills a human being is to be put to death. You are to have the same law for the foreigner and the native-born. I am the LORD your God. (Leviticus 24:17-22).*

The Quran also teaches the doctrine of retribution. Three of the world's major religions, and a large segment of the world's population, subscribe to the doctrine of retribution. That's kind of scary. This does not bode

---

[72] Bergen, Peter (2006). What Were the Causes of 9/11? Prospect Magazine, September 24, 2006.

well for a turnaround to Jesus' way of thinking. Extremists on all fronts: Christian, Jewish, and Muslim, will continue to use their sacred writings as a catalyst for violence. But this is a book about listening to Jesus, listening to the Word made flesh; and that Word is the opposite of the doctrine of retribution. Everyone gets to keep their eyes and their teeth. There are other ways to resolve our conflicts.

In America we still have the death penalty in over half of the states. We are not "united" on that one. Our federal government and our military branches can also exact punishment by calling for the death penalty. In contrast, 48 out of 50 European countries have abolished the death penalty. In a part of the world where fewer people per capita go to church on Sunday mornings than in America, there is more of a tendency to follow Jesus on this one. Jesus' call to non-violence here is something that needs to be a part of our social discourse on subjects like war and the death penalty. If it is not; if we leave Jesus locked up in the church for our private affairs only, then the Word is not allowed to be made flesh, and we are living at odds with the Word of God.

This Christmas season I watched the 1945 film *The Bells of St. Mary's* starring Bing Crosby as Father O'Malley, a priest in a new parish; and Ingrid Bergman as Sister Mary Benedict, the head nun who had run the parish school for quite some time. One of the school children, Eddie, gets pretty badly beaten up by another boy at school. Father O'Malley's response to Eddie was, "I like to see a man who can take care of himself." Sister Benedict tried to tell Eddie that she was proud of him, and that he did the right thing by turning the other cheek, and I thought to myself, "Hey, way to go, Sister! You're teaching that child the Word of God. You're encouraging that young one to live like Jesus." But then, sure enough, before you know it she was at the sporting goods store picking up a book on pugilism with every intention of teaching Eddie how to box; which she proceeded to do. It made for good humor, but once again totally bypassed Jesus with a preference for the cultural norm. The film is still a great film, and I can still recommend it as long as you watch it with Jesus' words firmly planted in your heart and mind.

This is an example of what I talked about earlier. We need to inject Jesus into our hearts and minds in such a way that whatever it is that we are listening to, watching, or reading at the moment will be subjected to our "Jesus processor." Just like our computers process information, filtering and sorting it based upon their programming, so we too need to process life by sorting out the myriad voices and comparing them to the one voice that matters—the voice of Jesus—the Word of God. If we invest ourselves in a long, slow, steady process of listening to Jesus on a regular basis we will eventually be unable to separate Jesus from our everyday, ordinary activities, including our entertainments. No moment of our day will be safe from the scrutiny of Jesus; and our lives will be better off because of it.

You see, I doubt that I can persuade anyone by simply writing a chapter in a book about Jesus' call to non-violence. Who am I, after all? Even Jesus himself could not persuade the Romans or the Jews not to use violence. The Romans crucified Jesus, and the Jews continued to try to win the battle against Rome by literally doing battle. I am speaking second hand when I tell you what Jesus says (third or fourth hand when you consider the process by which his words make their way to us in the 21st century). But if you are willing to listen directly to Jesus, and continue to do so over a long period of time, you will be convinced to make different decisions in your dealings with the world around you. You will find yourself voting differently, conversing differently about various issues, and using your time differently. You will be surprised how much of a difference listening to The Word of God can make in your life. Just reading The Bible will do little to deter violence. There's plenty of violence in The Bible, but Jesus will have nothing to do with it.

Having said that, I know he got angry. There was that whole getting upset at the Temple thing. He had his "moments." He may have even had regrets, as we do sometimes. Jesus was human, and that very fact paves the way for us to aspire to be like him. If he were not human I would not be writing this book, for I would have no case to make for the Word of God being something other than a book. The Word of God is a human being. God speaks through a human being. That means that God can speak through you, and through me, and through even the least likely people in the world. The people we fear, or despise, or even hate could very well be conduits through which God chooses to speak. You never know. How will we know? By listening to Jesus and comparing notes.

People who engage in social protest are often treated like criminals, even if they are engaging in acts of non-violence. The resent "Occupy Movement" has resulted in many arrests, as well as blatant use of pepper spray and rubber bullets in order to "control" the protesters. By being non-violent in a violent society you might find yourself a victim of violence, or a prisoner. One such social protester that comes to my mind here in America, an ancestor to those young people protesting today, is Daniel Berrigan.

Daniel Berrigan was born in Virginia, Minnesota, a blue collar mining community in the northeastern part of the state known as The Range, or 'Da Range' if you are from there. When he graduated high school he joined the Jesuits and in 1952 joined the priesthood. In the late 60s and early 70s he was called to teach and administrate at various educational institutions, including Cornell. It was during these years that he also began to actively protest the war in Viet Nam (another unnecessary war). He was one of the Catonsville Nine, a group of protestors who burned 378 draft files in the parking lot of the Catonsville Draft Board on May 17, 1968. He was arrested and sentenced to three years in prison. He was released in 1972.

On September 9, 1980 Berrigan, his brother Phillip, and six others formed the Plowshares movement. They trespassed onto a General Electric Nuclear Weapons facility and destroyed several warhead nose cones. They also ritually poured blood onto several documents and files related to the government's contract with G.E. Once again Berrigan was arrested. You can call him a radical if you like, or a nutcase. But to this day we are sitting on a stockpile of nuclear weapons that have enough firepower to destroy the planet many times over (and those are just the ones here in America). Their little ritual 30 years ago reminds us that we do not need to manufacture such weapons any more than we might need to use them. Berrigan and his compatriots were speaking The Word of God through their actions. They were doing what Jesus would do in a similar situation. Berrigan was no one special; just a kid from 'Da Range' in northern Minnesota. God can speak through anyone, anytime, anywhere.

On December 22, 2010 the United States and Russia, two of the world's nuclear superpowers, agreed to dismantle 650 nuclear weapons each, drawing down their nuclear arsenals to 1550 per country. The vote for approval of this agreement was 71-26.[73] One must wonder what was going on with the 26. The 3100 nuclear warheads that will remain active in our two countries have enough force to destroy humankind 31 times over, simply put.[74] There is much more to learn about the destructive force of

---

[73] http://www.wagingpeace.org/articles/1997/00/00_babst_consequences.php

[74] Oliphant, James and Muskal, Michael (2010). Senate Passes New START Treaty. Los Angeles Times, December 22, 2010.

nuclear weapons at the link listed here (footnote #5). I can't imagine anyone making a case that this is not enough firepower for a strong defense.

Jesus did not live in a world with nuclear weapons, so this is the closest we can come, biblically speaking, to commentary about such an issue. He did live in that part of the world which at the time was home to the world's one and only superpower. Rome was to Jesus' day what the U.S., Russia, and China are to our day. Rome was the big bully to whom Jesus was asking his followers to turn their cheeks. Rome was quite simply the enemy, one of the enemies we shall hear Jesus refer to in chapter nine.

We all want to live in a world free of war, free of nuclear weapons, free of hatred and turmoil. We all want to live in peace. Jesus offers us such peace, but we cannot have it without changing our way of life. We cannot continue the status quo and have what The Word of God so deeply desires for us. Jesus' last words in this section of Matthew refer to the path we need to walk; his words encapsulate succinctly the means by which we can get from point A to point B. Jesus says it in two words. "Live generously." Jesus was about giving himself away. He did not own anything—no possessions. Therefore nothing possessed him. We are told time and time again that what military might is all about is protecting what we have. Perhaps we need to think more about giving it all away rather than fighting so hard to protect it.

Chapter Nine

Who Loves You, Baby?

"You're familiar with the old written law, 'Love your friend,' and its unwritten companion, 'Hate your enemy.' I'm challenging that. I'm telling you to love your enemies. Let them bring out the best in you, not the worst. When someone gives you a hard time, respond with the energies of prayer, for then you are working out of your true selves, your God-created selves. This is what God does. He gives his best—the sun to warm and the rain to nourish—to everyone, regardless: the good and bad, the nice and nasty. If all you do is love the lovable, do you expect a bonus? Anybody can do that. If you simply say hello to those who greet you, do you expect a medal? Any run-of-the-mill sinner does that. (Matthew 5:43-47).

It begins with the Abramic Covenant (he was not yet called Abraham when God made these promises to him). It can be found in Genesis 12 & 13. God made promises to Abraham. One of those promises was land, and with it wealth.

God told Abram: "Leave your country, your family, and your father's home for a land that I will show you.

I'll make you a great nation
and bless you.

95

I'll make you famous;
you'll be a blessing.
I'll bless those who bless you;
those who curse you I'll curse.
All the families of the Earth
will be blessed through you."

So Abram left just as God said, and Lot left with him. Abram was seventy-five years old when he left Haran. Abram took his wife Sarai and his nephew Lot with him, along with all the possessions and people they had gotten in Haran, and set out for the land of Canaan and arrived safe and sound.

Abram passed through the country as far as Shechem and the Oak of Moreh. At that time the Canaanites occupied the land.

God appeared to Abram and said, "I will give this land to your children." Abram built an altar at the place God had appeared to him. (Genesis 12:1-7).

Abram stayed on the move in faithfulness to God. Chapter 13 begins, "So Abram left Egypt and went back to the Negev, he and his wife and everything he owned, and Lot still with him. By now Abram was very rich, loaded with cattle and silver and gold." (Genesis 13:1-2). The Old Testament, the "Bible" of Jesus, includes a story that sends a clear message. It is a simple message that makes perfect sense. We even have a common, everyday maxim that summarizes it. We say, "You scratch my back and I'll scratch yours." You do for me and I'll do for you. This is the way human beings function socially. It is understood; an unwritten contract.

I recently sent an appreciation gift to someone who has provided leadership in the congregation that I serve. One day that person called me and implied that she would need to reciprocate in some way. But this was not the spirit in which the gift was given. We are wired that way. Someone gives us something and we want to give them something back. Of course, the opposite could also be true, "If you don't scratch my back I will let you itch and itch and itch." Those who don't give will not get in return. This is how we think. This is how we function. This makes sense to us. It is the way the world works.

So it also makes sense to us that those who are faithful to God, like Abram, will receive blessings from God. Today there is a segment of the Christian population in America that subscribes to the philosophy that wealth is the end result of being a good and faithful Christian, the so-called Prosperity Gospel. This Prosperity Gospel fits well in a Capitalist society that holds to the American Dream. Churches that subscribe to it are successful by economic standards. They worship in large and beautifully appointed buildings. They excel in opulence. And, as its proponents would claim, all of this has its roots in The Bible, in Old Testament literature. Jesus knew this was part of his tradition. He might have gone to synagogue and heard the following:

> *My question: What are God-worshipers like?*
> *Your answer: Arrows aimed at God's bull's-eye.*

> *They settle down in a promising place;*
> *Their kids inherit a prosperous farm. (Psalm 25:12-13).*

You scratch God's back and God will scratch yours. It makes sense. It is the way we do business. This idea is perfectly marketable. But Jesus says,

"This is what God does. He gives his best—the sun to warm and the rain to nourish—to everyone, regardless: the good and bad, the nice and nasty." This too makes sense, if you take a moment to think about. Some of the wealthiest people in the world couldn't give a hang about God. Some of the poorest people in the world are the most faithful toward God. And by the way, Jesus was poor. Jesus chose to be poor. He's the one that brought up that whole camel through the eye of a needle thing.

One of the most haunting texts for me in the Gospels is when a rich young man approaches Jesus asking how he might inherit eternal life, (I suppose he thought he could simply buy it). This text haunts me because by global standards I too am rich. My privilege is a consequence of my life path, my good fortune. It has nothing to do with my faithfulness to God. Here is the text from Mark.

> *As Jesus started on his way, a man ran up to him and fell on his knees before him. "Good teacher," he asked, "what must I do to inherit eternal life?"*

> *"Why do you call me good?" Jesus answered. "No one is good—except God alone. You know the commandments: 'You shall not murder, you shall not commit adultery, you shall not steal, you shall not give false testimony, you shall not defraud, honor your father and mother.'"*

> *"Teacher," he declared, "all these I have kept since I was a boy."*

> *Jesus looked at him and loved him. "One thing you lack," he said. "Go, sell everything you have and give to the poor, and you will have treasure in heaven. Then come, follow me."*

At this the man's face fell. He went away sad, because he had great wealth.

Jesus looked around and said to his disciples, "How hard it is for the rich to enter the kingdom of God!"

The disciples were amazed at his words. But Jesus said again, "Children, how hard it is[e] to enter the kingdom of God! 25 It is easier for a camel to go through the eye of a needle than for someone who is rich to enter the kingdom of God." (Mark 10:17-25).

Oh yeah, and there it is, that camel through the needle's eye thing. Notice that the young man's inability to follow Jesus had nothing to do with his wealth. He would keep his wealth. Sure, he was faithful to God. He was good at keeping the commandments, etc. But this is Mark's gospel, and following Jesus is the kind of faithfulness Mark is most interested in. This is a young man who missed a valuable opportunity, a young man who did not, like the disciples, drop everything in order to follow Jesus. In fact Mark (and Luke who tells this same story in his 18th chapter), want their readers to know that wealth is an impediment to following Jesus. So it is just the opposite of the prosperity gospel. Why would someone who claims to follow Jesus want more of the things that make it that much harder to follow Jesus?

The economy of God's Kingdom according to The Word of God is not what we expect. Everybody gets what they get. It has nothing to do with faith or faithfulness. It has nothing to do with being a "good" person or a "bad" person. It just is, like the rain and the sun. The weather is the weather. It can be terrible where you are one day and beautiful where you are the next. The planet spins and the weather changes. There is nothing we can do about it; and likely nothing God can do about it. It is what it is. There is equity and justice built into the system—God's system called Creation. The Jesus follower needs to accept what is, and not get caught up in the illusion of control so prevalent in our religious banter; the illusion that God will "bend" the rules for any one particular individual or group.

As for the loving your enemy stuff, I'm not sure where the hate your enemy thing comes from. Perhaps it is from Deuteronomy.

> *God wasn't attracted to you and didn't choose you because you were big and important—the fact is, there was almost nothing to you. He did it out of sheer love, keeping the promise he made to your ancestors. God stepped in and mightily bought you back out of that world of slavery, freed you from the iron grip of Pharaoh king of Egypt. Know this: God, your God, is God indeed, a God you can depend upon. He keeps his covenant of loyal love with those who love him and observe his commandments for a thousand generations. But he also pays back those who hate him, pays them the wages of death; he isn't slow to pay them off—those who hate him, he pays right on time.*

> *So keep the command and the rules and regulations that I command you today. Do them.*

> *And this is what will happen: When you, on your part, will obey these directives, keeping and following them, God, on his part, will keep the covenant of loyal love that he made with your ancestors:*

> *He will love you,*
>
> *he will bless you,*
>
> *he will increase you. (Deuteronomy 7:7-12).*

God loves those who love Him. God sticks it to those who hate Him. This is yet another example of back-scratching theology. This is the God Jesus grew up with. How did he get this other notion? Who knows? This is what makes Jesus, Jesus. Plus, we have here again fodder for the prosperity gospel—God will "increase" those who are faithful. I suppose it stands to reason that people would read in their Bibles that God hates the foreigner, the enemy, the "other," and then deduce that it is okay to destroy these folks. Get out your pitchforks and torches! We're going after the bastards! This fits well the retribution doctrine we reflected on earlier. This is the danger of reading The Bible without taking Jesus along for the ride. We run the risk of living in opposition to the way Jesus calls us to live.

It all fits together so neatly. It all makes such good sense. Jesus' worldview clashed with the popular worldview of his day, and still clashes with the popular worldview of our day. You crush your enemies. You give back only when you get. You get blessed when you're good. Remember Santa Claus?—"You better watch out, you better not cry, you better not pout . . . Santa Claus is coming to town." For some Jesus is sort of modern day Santa Claus. The doctrine of the Second Coming fits well with this. I once saw a T-Shirt in one of those iron-on shops that read, "Jesus is coming again, and boy is he pissed!" Jesus, the righteous judge of that doctrine, is going to stick it to the enemy, stick it to the unfaithful; he will stick it to all the bad, bad people. It makes sense. It is the way the world works, (or rather, doesn't work).

This is not the Jesus of Matthew's gospel, at least not in this chapter. This Jesus must be crazy, telling us not to stick it to our enemies. This Jesus tells us to love our enemies. This Jesus tells us we get the sunny days and the good life regardless of our faithfulness to God. Jesus tells us about a God that loves everyone the same. God loves Christians, Jews, Muslims, Buddhists, Hindus and Atheists alike. It just doesn't make any sense. Do we really want to follow a guy that teaches such nonsense? I, for one, *do* want to follow this guy; and it'll be a little easier to do so when more of us try to follow him together. We must stop being so loyal to the conventional wisdom that we wallow in every day. We must un-tie and un-gag Jesus from inside of our churches and let him speak. He is The Word of God. God wants us to listen to him, and risk being crazy right along with him.

But instead we try to fit Jesus into what makes sense, into what we know to be the norm. We keep going to war; keep hating our enemies; keep trying to soak life for all we can get from it; keep praying to God to manipulate the weather, our health, and our wealth for our benefit. Maybe we want God to just be a Sugar Daddy in the sky. Maybe that is all we want from our religion. Jesus will not abide this. He will walk away from this; or rather we will walk away from him, like that rich young man. We have a choice.

This crazy Jesus; this Word of God is someone we are called into relationship with. If we are Christian, then this call is real. The church has made it optional by muddying the waters between God and Jesus and the Holy Spirit. The people I serve quite often think of them all as one and the same, a byproduct of trying to understand an impossible conundrum called *The Trinity*. Don't ask me to explain that one. I can't. And I'm a pastor!!

For Christians, "being spiritual" means being in a relationship with Jesus—not just being in a relationship with God or with the Holy Spirit. This Jesus is a figure of historical record . . . our spiritual lives are grounded in a reality external to ourselves—something that we are not able to manipulate or fashion to our design (at least, not easily). This gives an integrity to our spirituality that basically keeps us honest . . . The Jesus of the Bible is God made accessible. To know God through Jesus is to be in relationship with someone who has been seen, heard, and touched.[75]

The ultimate question for those of us who already call ourselves Christian is whether or not we want to follow this guy. It seems strange to need to pose this question, but that is where we are at. We find ourselves with churches that are not so full anymore, not so full of people who grew up believing in Jesus rather than responding to a call to follow Jesus. How do we make this transition? Can we make this transition? Do we need to? Jesus never walked into the synagogue and said, "Follow me." He roamed the country-side, went to the local bars, and walked into people's work environments calling people to follow. We only need a few in our churches who understand this call. The call to follow happens when this crazy guy named Jesus gets out into the streets, out into politics, out into businesses, out into homes, out into schools, out into bars and casinos and all of the other places we would least expect to find Jesus. The Word of God is waiting to be unleashed upon the world, the real world we live in day in and day out. And the way that Word is unleashed is through you and through me when that Word lives in us.

---

[75] Powell, p. 27

This following of Jesus will not be easy. There is real risk involved. There is a real cross to be born. It is not the cross of Jesus; it is your cross and mine. I wear a cross regularly. If you ask I will tell you that it is unabashedly *my* cross that I carry around my neck, the cross that I carry into every situation in my life. I take it off most of the time at home, but I am even rethinking that as I write this. I guess you could say that even when I sit down to watch a football game or a movie, that cross is still there because the consciousness that accompanies my cross is still in play. I do not leave Jesus in my dresser drawer at night. He is indelibly etched in my heart and mind; he is part of my DNA. I will not shake him off so easily.

Each of us will need to decide to what extent we will let Jesus possess us, the degree to which we will let Jesus take over our lives. It will be inconvenient, uncomfortable, and even downright frustrating at times. Jesus will call us beyond our norms, beyond business as usual, beyond the status quo, beyond cultural conformity, beyond what we know, beyond what we want, beyond what we think is important, beyond the life we have come to know and love. There will be times when we will say, "Come on, Jesus; really? You want me to do that?"

> *On the road someone asked if he could go along. "I'll go with you, wherever," he said.*

> *Jesus was curt: "Are you ready to rough it? We're not staying in the best inns, you know."*

> *Jesus said to another, "Follow me."*

> *He said, "Certainly, but first excuse me for a couple of days, please. I have to make arrangements for my father's funeral."*

Jesus refused. "First things first. Your business is life, not death. And life is urgent: Announce God's kingdom!"

Then another said, "I'm ready to follow you, Master, but first excuse me while I get things straightened out at home."

Jesus said, "No procrastination. No backward looks. You can't put God's kingdom off till tomorrow. Seize the day." (Luke 9:57-61).

Harsh? Unreasonable? Unfeeling? Uncompromising? Following Jesus will require us to take unpopular stands, like protesting against war when the majority that rules thinks otherwise; like loving the people our communities ostracize; like forgiving when the state has ruled to fry someone in the electric chair or end their life by lethal injection; like confronting people who spew forth racial slurs in the form of seemingly innocent jokes; like welcoming the stranger and giving until we have no more to give. Hearing The Word of God involves this kind of responsiveness to The Word of God—to Jesus. Every minute of every hour of every day of our lives we must decide again and again whether or not we will respond to that Word and follow. This is the crux of the Christian life.

Chapter Ten

The Last Word

"In a word, what I'm saying is, grow up. You're kingdom subjects. Now live like it. Live out your God-created identity. Live generously and graciously toward others, the way God lives toward you." (Matthew 5:48).

There is an interesting dynamic, a set-up if you will, in organized religion; and specifically in the Christian Church. As a professional serving a local congregation I reside right at the heart of it. The set-up is that I am supported by donations made by our congregation's members. Our budget supports benevolence, but only to a minor degree. Embarrassed by the fact, I am painfully aware each year at annual meeting time that the majority of our congregational budget goes to support—well—me. I have spoken with other clergy who feel this way too. Religious donations and the livelihoods of clergy are intertwined. Therein lays the set-up.

The budget also funds the upkeep of our beautiful building. The congregation I serve now has a gorgeous worship space, a worship space they take much pride in. There is no doubt that the space provides for us a transport to an alternate reality, as if we have indeed entered the realm of the Most High on Sunday mornings. I am grateful to serve this congregation, and I love them all dearly. But we live together in the midst of this set-up. It is hard to process this in light of Jesus' call.

I end up time and time again with the awareness that this is the place to which Jesus has called me, for better or for worse, for richer or for poorer. My people feel this way too, so that's a good thing. It won't always make sense, this following; this response to Jesus' call. I get that. But the set-up is still there, and another reason why the institutional church struggles to survive into the 21st century.

My Lutheran roots are founded upon an historic event called The Reformation. This began as one man's campaign to call the Church, the Holy Roman Church of his day, into question. What we have today is the plethora of "children" born out of that event, the myriad denominations, or non-denominations that pepper the Christian landscape. Martin Luther began that campaign by nailing 95 Theses to the door of the Castle Church in Wittenberg in 1517. In this decade we will celebrate the 500th anniversary of that event. I think we will celebrate that anniversary with a strong sense that a new Reformation is afoot.

Matthew Fox has posited his 95 Theses in his book *A New Reformation: Creation Spirituality and the Transformation of Christianity*. Many others, some of whom I have quoted in this book (Borg, Crossan, Levine, Spong, etc.) are taking part in the creation of the next wave of Christianity. How this wave will affect the "set-up" I do not know. There is inherent in this new wave a call to do what *The Word of God* says here in this last piece of Matthew 5; to grow up!

This is a time for Christian leaders to first call themselves to maturity in the following of The Word of God, and then to call those they serve to the same. We cannot continue to coddle our constituents in fear of losing them and their money. The set-up is that anytime someone's toes get stepped on in the congregation they will walk, after their toes stop aching.

Our leaders walk on egg-shells because their jobs are on the line. We need leaders whose integrity is tied to their hearing of the Word of God; tied to their faithfulness to Jesus, the Living Word. We need leaders who will listen and call their people to do the same. Every congregational decision should rightly be prefaced by the question, "What does The Word of God have to say?" Which is to say, "What does Jesus have to say?"

This is the beginning of the "growing up" that needs to take place. Each one of our congregants must be encouraged to stand toe to toe with Jesus, to answer to Jesus—not to boards and committees. Jesus needs to be the place where the buck stops, not the Annual Meeting or the Church Council, not the Synod or the Bishop's Office, unless of course the Meeting and the Council and the Synod and The Bishop have as their bottom line Jesus, The Word of God.

We have spent these pages together hopefully finding compelling reasons to listen to the Word and to follow the Word. This is what I believe to be the primary task of Christians in the 21st century. We have spent the past 500 years building our churches and doing whatever it is we have done in them. We have been in our proverbial kindergarten long enough now. It is time to grow up. It is time for all of us to respond to the call, to engage in *lectio divina* and other practices that lead us closer to The Word of God. It is time for each one of us to take personal responsibility to do the work required in order to assimilate the Word of God into our lives.

Jesus calls us "kingdom subjects" and encourages us to live in accordance with our kingdom status. The kingdom of God is something Jesus refers to a lot in his ministry. The term "kingdom of God" is exclusive to the New Testament, and pretty well isolated in Matthew, Mark, Luke and Acts. The one passage that brings the concept home for me is in Luke.

Jesus, grilled by the Pharisees on when the kingdom of God would come, answered, "The kingdom of God doesn't come by counting the days on the calendar. Nor when someone says, 'Look here!' or, 'There it is!' And why? Because God's kingdom is already among you." (Luke 17:20-21).

There is also a companion version in the Gospel of Thomas, which is my favorite of the two. After all, The Gospel of Thomas is as much The Word of God as any other gospel, since it reflects very directly the voice of Jesus. Long before Luke wrote the words quoted above, these words were passed on to Jesus followers in the early first century.

Jesus said: If your leaders say to you, "Look! The Kingdom is in the sky!" then the birds will be there before you are. If they say that the Kingdom is in the sea, then the fish will be there before you. Rather the Kingdom is within you and it is outside of you. (Gospel of Thomas 3a)[76]

The Kingdom of God is not a place, an identifiable location. The Kingdom of God is not a place we go exclusively when we die. The Church, or any particular religious institution, is not the path to the Kingdom of God. The Kingdom of God is a state of being, a mindset, and a frame of reference. The Kingdom of God is what those who have ears to hear, hear; and what those who have eyes to see, see. The Kingdom of God is what happens when The Word of God infiltrates our consciousness and transforms it to perceive the world as Jesus would perceive it. Most importantly, the Kingdom of God happens when the battle between our

---

[76]   Davies, The Gospel of Thomas, p. 5

egos and the mind of Christ is won by the Word of God, by the heart and mind of Jesus.

The Word of God points the way to the Kingdom of God, lays out the path, sets the boundaries, defines the ground-rules, makes the crooked paths straight and the rough places a plain. We use the term "Kingdom of God" because Jesus used the term. He defined it on his terms and we have re-defined it on our own terms.

> *The kingdom of God means, then, the ruling of God in our hearts; it means those principles which separate us off from the kingdom of the world and the devil; it means the benign sway of grace; it means the Church as that Divine institution whereby we may make sure of attaining the spirit of Christ and so win that ultimate kingdom of God where He reigns without end in "the holy city, the New Jerusalem, coming down out of heaven from God" (Revelation 21:2).*[77]

This definition starts out okay but ultimately points back to the institutional church as "that Divine institution whereby we may make sure of attaining the spirit of Christ and so win that ultimate kingdom of God." The church just loves to retain that "hook" so that people are led to believe that the institution *is* the path to God's Kingdom. And I am not just picking on the Catholics here. Lutherans, Anglicans, Presbyterians, Methodists, Baptists, et al.; all of our Christian religious institutions love to play the trump card that will attach constituents to their organizations. This is a bastardization of one of Jesus' core teachings. It is true that someone may encounter the Kingdom of God within the confines of a church, but the church is not the path. The Word of God is the path, and

---

[77] Pope, H. (1910). Kingdom of God. In The Catholic Encyclopedia. New York: Robert Appleton Company.

Jesus is that Word. Getting this straightened out somehow is a big part of the growing up we need to do.

Access to the Kingdom of God is like access to breath. Jesus teaches that it is within us and all around us—oxygen. There is only one thing we need to do to acquire oxygen. We have to breathe; we must inhale. We must also exhale to release carbon dioxide that would poison our systems if it built up without the proper balance of oxygen. Breathing in and breathing out are foundational to life itself. Inhaling the living, breathing Word of God, and exhaling whatever it is in our lives that stands in the way of that Word is the process, the way we enter the Kingdom. It is that simple, and that complex. It is accessible to everyone. Anyone with ears to hear can obtain access anywhere, anytime. There are no other requirements, institutional or otherwise.

> *It is not a place, of course, but a condition. Kingship might be a better word. "Thy kingdom come, thy will be done," Jesus prayed. The two are in apposition.*

> *Insofar as here and there, and now and then, God's kingly will is being done in various and odd ways among us even at this moment, the kingdom has come already.*

> *Insofar as all the odd ways we do his will at this moment are at best half-baked and halfhearted, the kingdom is still a long way off.*

> *Jesus is maybe at his best in describing the feeling you get when you glimpse the Thing itself—It's like finding a million dollars in a field, he says, or a jewel worth a king's ransom. It's like finding something you hated to lose and thought you'd never find again . . .*

When the kingdom really comes, it's as if the thing you lost and thought you'd never find again is you.[78]

At best, then, the Kingdom of God comes and goes, just like the Word of God in our lives. We catch glimpses of it all, and have experiences that make it so very real, only to have it all slip into non-existence a moment later and wonder where it could have gone. However, when we do find ourselves there, right smack dab in the middle of it, we are in that moment growing just a little older as "kingdom subjects," a little wiser by Jesus standards. In that moment our eyes see a little clearer, and our ears hear a little more acutely. We are growing up!

We grow up by "living out our God-created identity." We grow up when we stop being who everyone else thinks we should be and focus on who Jesus is calling us to be. It is like that last line from Buechner; "When the kingdom really comes, it's as if the thing you lost and thought you'd never find again is you." When we grow up we discover that the integrity forged in us by the Spirit of Jesus himself is real, and does not need corroboration by any systems of power or authority figures. The woman who started the food pantry knew this was her calling. Oh sure, she had to navigate the waters of building use and asking for donations and publicity, but I know she was confident that this was her calling, and that there would indeed be a food pantry. (In fact, there now is a food pantry). There is an audacity that comes from growing into God's Kingdom; that comes from letting The Word of God be our primary guiding principle. We know who we are, and that we belong to a group of global disciples who will let nothing get in the way of that guiding principle.

---

[78] Buechner, pp. 49-50

Finally there is the conscription to "Live generously and graciously toward others, the way God lives toward you." If you do nothing else, either as a result of reading this book or in spite of it, then for Jesus' sake do this. Whomever the "other" is to you—the Gay or the Lesbian, the Black or the Hispanic, the Muslim or the Hindu, the town drunk or the guy whose mulberry bush encroaches your yard—live graciously and generously toward him or her. This is a great way to begin to experience life in the Kingdom of God, and to flesh out The Word of God made real in Jesus.

I end where I began, with that children's song; only with a slightly different lyric. I hope you too can sing this song with the same gusto as those kids sing the traditional version. I also hope that one day they too will sing this new version with the same gusto, and understand why they no longer sing the old version.

He's J-E-S-U-S

The One who loves the best

I fill my life with The Word of God

He's J-E-S-U-S

Appendix—
On Scrumptious Scriptures

When I accepted my new call a few years ago I started right away with lection divina. I call it *Scrumptious Scriptures* (see Eugene Peterson's book *Eat This Book*). Here is how I lead Scrumptious Scriptures. I gather together small groups of *disciples*, people who are really interested in listening to what Jesus has to say. Over the period of one hour we read a text, a Jesus text. I use Jesus material almost exclusively because I want people to have a Jesus encounter, a direct interaction with The Word of God. This is not a time for theological discourse. It is time to hear The Word and let that Word soak into our hearts and minds, seep into our very lives.

The process once we gather is simple. It is important to stay on task, and important to stress the need for confidentiality at the outset. There are three primary steps that begin after an opening prayer. I encourage people in the group to pray. This, too, is part of growing up. After the prayer one person reads the text out loud from their preferred translation. This reading is followed by one minute of silence. This reading and silence gives the group the opportunity to reflect upon the first of three tasks, *to listen for a word or phrase that speaks the loudest to them personally.* In other words, this is the time to identify that piece of the text that resonates to you. It may be different from what resonates to others, or it may be the same. The one minute of silence is followed by a simple reporting to the group what that word or phrase is for each one in the group. This is not a time for analysis. Just a simple reporting will do.

Next, someone else reads the text from a different translation. As the group listens,[79] and as the group enters the now two minutes of silence, *the members of the group need to ask themselves how the text is speaking to where they are living their lives in the here and now. What is going on in his or her life that this text addresses? What little corner of my life is Jesus pointing to as he speaks? How is Jesus responding to me directly in the life I am living?* After the two minutes of silence people can share with the group what awareness they have. It is easy for people to lean on generalities and theological discussion. As a leader it is important to encourage people to get "intimate" with the text, reminding them that confidentiality is the bedrock of the group.

The third and last task in Scrumptious Scriptures is *to reflect upon how The Word of God is encouraging change in each of us. What will be different for me in my life because I have spent an hour in Scrumptious Scriptures on this particular day? Jesus is calling me beyond something in my life. What is that something?* The text is read a third time from yet another translation. The reading is followed by three to five minutes of silence. Following the silence people are encouraged to share with the group the thing they will focus on changing in their lives. Again, it is important not to get too lost in generalities. Be as specific as possible. Make sure the change is achievable and real.

---

[79] I encourage listening to the text being read rather than following along in your Bible.

Someone in the group is then asked to close with prayer. In some groups that have been together for a long period of time and where trust is high you may want to pray for each other in some way. After prayer Scrumptious Scriptures is over for the time being, always to be approached again another day. I occasionally have a few months that go by without running a group after two years in my current parish. I am growing uncomfortable with such lapses and am seriously considering making Scrumptious Scriptures as regular and ordinary as our weekly worship. My thinking as I write this is to schedule it a couple of times weekly and make sure it stays on the schedule no matter what. Perhaps, over time, this could grow to be like daily prayer. It is as much about my willingness to commit as a leader as it is about the people's willingness to commit. At any rate, I have written my intentions here, thus establishing some form of accountability. I am still working on growing up. I only hope I will always have others who are willing to grow up right along with me.

Bibliography

Barclay, William (1975). The Gospel of Matthew, Volume 1. Westminster Press.

Barr, James (1980. The Scope and Authority of the Bible. Westminster.

Bergen, Peter (2006). What Were the Causes of 9/11? Prospect Magazine, September 24, 2006.

Borg, Marcus J.(2006). Jesus: Uncovering the Life, Teachings, and Relevance of a Religious Revolutionary. Harper.

Brueggemann, Walter (2010). The Word That Redescribes the World. Fortress.

Buber, Martin I and Thou (1958). trans. Ronald Gregor Smith. New York: Scribner.

Buechner, Frederich (1973). Wishful Thinking: A Theological ABC. Harper & Row.

Carlin, George (1998) Brain Droppings. Hyperion.

Clarke-Stewart, Alison (2007). Divorce: Causes and Consequences: Current Perspectives in Psychology. Yale University Press.

Crossley, James G. (2010). The New Testament and Jewish Law: A Guide for the Perplexed. T &T Clark.

Davies, Stevan (2002). The Gospel of Thomas Annotated & Explained, Translated and annotated by Stevan Davies; Forward by Andrew Harvey. Skylight Paths Publishing.

Evangelical Lutheran Worship, Pew Edition copyright 2006, Augsburg Fortress, Publishers.

Funk, Robert W. (1996). Honest to Jesus. Harper.

Hanh, Thich Nhat (1995). Living Buddha, Living Christ. Riverhead Books.

Levine, Amy-Jill (2006). The Misunderstood Jew: The Church and the Scandal of the Jewish Jesus. Harper.

Luther, M. (1999, c1971). Vol. 47: Luther's works, vol. 47 : The Christian in Society IV (J. J. Pelikan, H. C. Oswald & H. T. Lehmann, Ed.).

Luther, M. (1999, c1967). Vol. 54: Luther's works, vol. 54 : Table Talk (J. J. Pelikan, H. C. Oswald & H. T. Lehmann, Ed.). Luther's Works (Vol. 54, Page 408). Philadelphia: Fortress Press.

MacCulloch, Diamaid (2009). Christianity: The First Three Thousand Years. Viking.

Mack, Burton L. (1995). Who Wrote the New Testament. Harper.

McKenna, Megan (2002) Matthew: The Book of Mercy. New City Press.

Meyers, Robin R. (2009). Saving Jesus from the Church: How to Stop Worshiping Christ and Start Following Jesus. Harper.

Morrow, Lance (2001). The Case for Rage and Retribution, Time Magazine, September 14, 2001.

New Revised Standard Version Bible, copyright 1989, Division of Christian Education of the National Council of the Churches of Christ in the United States of America.

O'Dell, Donald L. (2006). How the Bible Became the Bible. Infinity Publishing.

Oliphant, James and Muskal, Michael (2010). Senate Passes New START Treaty. Los Angeles Times, December 22, 2010.

Peterson, Eugene H. (2006). Eat This Book: A Conversation in the Art of Spiritual Reading. William B. Eerdmans.

Peterson, Eugene H. (2005). Christ Plays in Ten Thousand Places: A Conversation in Spiritual Theology. William B. Eerdmans.

Peterson, Eugene H. (2000). A Long Obedience in the Same Direction: Discipleship in an Instant Society. IVP Books, 2nd ed.

Peterson, Eugene H. (2002). The Message: The Bible in Contemporary Language. Colorado Springs: NavPress.

Pope, H. (1910). Kingdom of God. In The Catholic Encyclopedia. New York: Robert Appleton Company.

Powell, Mark Allan (2004). Loving Jesus. Fortress Press.

Putnam, Robert D. and Campbell, David E. (2010). Walking away from church. Los Angeles Times, October 27, 2010.

Shaia, Alexander J. (2010). The Hidden Power of the Gospels: Four Question, Four Paths, One Journey. Harper.

Tappert, T. G. (2000, c1959). The Book of Concord : The Confessions of the Evangelical Lutheran Church. The Small Catechism: I, 4). Philadelphia: Fortress Press.

CPSIA information can be obtained at www.ICGtesting.com
Printed in the USA
LVOW040623030512

280174LV00002B/148/P